BA
PIGEON

It's Rare To See One, And It's Rare To Find True Love Online

By
Matt Bird

.

DEDICATION

To the person who taught me:
"Winners are grinners in life."

CONTENTS

This book is by Matt Bird and it is about the quest for love. Matt has always loved a bit of poetry and music, so he thought he'd write something about his romantic experiences. If his life was put into a power ballad, the opening lyrics to Gloria Gaynor's *I Will Survive* would read like this. Please do sing along:

His first time was in a metro, he was terrified
He told her he was experienced, but he kind of lied
She was a big girl, and there's something you should know
I think he stuck it in her belly button, but hey it's still a hole

So, he wrote a book, about his life
His search for love and his online dating strife
He's got quite a story to tell and some of it's a bit crass
Including one and half one-night stands and two fingers up his...
He did SURVIVE!

SECTION ONE:

BY WAY OF INTRODUCTION

A welcome note from Matt Bird

Hello and welcome to my book about love. Well, I say love, but since I am still single, it is really a book about trying to find it rather than about having it. In the 21ˢᵗ century, this is known as dating, and the rules of dating seem to change faster than the average person can take a selfie, edit it, add a filter and upload to a dating website. From Tinder to Sugardaddy.com, millions of us are searching for a human connection. Whether for one night or for an entire lifetime, satisfying our hearts, minds and bodies is something that consumes us all.

I'm Matt, and I'm a mid-forties bachelor from a small town in Devon; it has a population of 30,000 people yet only five different surnames. Despite the rumours of rural in-breeding, I have the predictable five digits on each hand and no webbing between my toes. But being from a small town has its problems. Let's just say all the good girls are taken. The ones who are left are single for a reason, even if the reason is just that they don't want to be with me! Hence, I turned to online dating.

I am the middle brother of three; we all had a rather wonderful childhood and still enjoy the company of our happily married parents. I own a successful company and now live near to my childhood home in the neighbouring county, Somerset. In many respects I am fortunate, but I still haven't found a special person to share it all with. (P.S. I did not lift this short introduction from my dating profile: any similarities to a particular profile are, in fact, coincidental.)

My dad is in part the inspiration for this book; he is a great role model and one of the bits of advice he has always repeated to me is, "Son, don't go looking for love, let love come to you!" I try to live by this mantra, but I am beginning to think that rather than being wise, he is just speaking literally. After all, he met my mother when he physically crashed into her on a flight of stairs at work. Beautifully, he says he knew immediately he wanted to marry her; he says their collision knocked the sense into him. Since love and marriage came easily to him, he might not be the best at this kind of advice. But saying that, in comparison with the advice given by my friend's parents, my dad is The Guru! Once, my mate's dad offered his best wisdom, which was to tell me to marry an ugly girl. He said, if she runs off, who cares?

You can just marry another one!

Following the kind of logic that says experience creates wisdom, I am a dating genius! With my extensive dating experience, I am the perfect person to hand out advice about dating – I mean, I consider myself a normal bloke, but my journey into online dating has been anything but normal. That being said, my cat, Smirnoff, keeps sending me withering looks as if he knows better. I'm pretty certain he despairs of me, but since I am the bringer of Felix, he continues to accept my failings. Besides, my cat taught me the real meaning of love. I realised this after he was tragically knocked over by a yellow metro. The vet miraculously put his head back on for the sum of £400 – and when I picked him up after surgery, in that worry-filled moment, I knew what love was. Ironically, I lost my virginity in a yellow metro, however, I don't think the two incidents are connected. But I will talk more about that later.

What I do know is that my brothers and I were raised the same, treated the same, and loved the same, but we have all turned out so different. Both brothers are settled down now, yet they are totally different to each other too. One is quite serious and religious, and the other is a little reckless and enjoys life a bit closer to the edge than I would say is comfortable. Although, I'm quite happy for him to continue with his wild lifestyle for a couple of reasons: firstly, he gives us all something to laugh about at family get-togethers, such as the time our mother walked into his bedroom with a plate of bangers and mash and he was taking a girl up the bum. I will come onto that (not literally) in a bit. Although I won't be divulging about my brother in the same conversation as the one about my pets. Secondly, while our family worry about him, they're not worrying about me. When I reflect on my family, I realise that luck and opportunity have so much to do with how things pan out.

While my reflections in this book are sometimes judgemental (Hey, I'm from Devon! What have we got if not lovely beaches, strangely similar foreheads and snappy skills of judging?) occasionally rude and frequently offensive, all stories are true. I have changed a few identities and switched things around to protect some identities and other egos.

Over the course of my online gambit, it would appear I have unknowingly appeared on dwarf-dating.com, disability-dating.org and hot-to-trot.com for people into horses, judging by some of the people I have met. Then there was the girl with the really large head who I would have described as a *Sniper's Dream*. However, I judge in jest. We cannot help who we love and we cannot help who we don't love. At the beating heart of things, I believe in reality we are all the same. This book is intended as a warm and positive book about looking for love, living with not finding it, and the constant angst of trying to work out who a perfect partner might be anyway. I mean, we all deserve love, but not all of us will find it.

Not online anyway!

THE POINT, THE PLACE AND

THE PEOPLE

Why do we need this book?

And why trust me?

The Point

You've chosen this book, so the *love* topic must be of interest. I'll give you the stats shortly, so you will know for certain your stress is real. But out of the millions of books available, why read this one?

I didn't start out as a dating expert. As you will read, I have had my fair share of long-term and short-term relationships, but as yet, I still haven't found my lobster. And now, at the grand old age of forty-something, I have clocked up many dating miles. My dating settings are well-calibrated and regularly serviced, so my service history provides good data for learning about dating. I can't promise to offer you the answers; what I can promise is to share my wisdom and my errors. I can also promise to share my diligent attention to detail.

My decision to write about dating, and to engage with social discourse and expectations of love, was born out of frustration. It's true to say that men also feel pressure to settle down, desire to create a family and a need to be loved. But, after another failed date, I found myself at a loss. Finally, I decided to start keeping a journal of my efforts. The final date that threw me into journal writing was with yet another nutter who clearly believed she was entirely normal. I'm pretty certain she should have had a carer with her full-time. I drove to Ilfracombe to meet her, which is a lovely town on the Devon coast, and as a fact it is probably irrelevant. But it was the only nice bit of the whole occasion. Not only did she turn up an hour late (in hindsight, I'd say more fool me for waiting) but she also turned up high on drugs.

In fact, she was a pretty good advert for why you should never do drugs. She told me she was different to other women; in fairness, I couldn't argue with this statement. To prove her uniqueness, she enthused about her belligerent behaviours. One example she proudly regaled occurred during the BSE scare (remember mad cow disease?). At this time, she stated, she bought loads of beef as it was going cheap since nobody would eat it. Surprised, I wondered out loud the scare hadn't put her off.

She replied, "Nope – I just put it in the freezer until the scare was over."

As I found an excuse to leave, I thought to myself,

maybe it wasn't the drugs after all!

The next day, like a male Bridget Jones, I bought a new journal and set up a new folder on my laptop. And here we are…

My relationship history has brought many comparisons to mind. Often, we compare to self-criticise, but I have found comfort in comparing. As you will see through my stories, my brothers and I are very different. Yet, our parents loved us all the same. We shared the same upbringing and were fortunate enough to be surrounded by stable and nurturing role models. Our differences have provided me much relief in my loneliest moments. As much as our lives are a result of our choices, they *must* also be affected by chance too.

But my ease is short-lived; I realise my single status might not be my fault, and there might be nothing wrong with me (except for my wandering eye, but I'll tell you more about that later), however, I still want a relationship. And this isn't just as a cure for loneliness. I recently saw an article in a newspaper which said people in relationships tend to live longer than those who are single. Apparently, we're just not allowed to stop and enjoy the single life without fear of death. I wondered, is singleness worse for you than smoking?

So, where life expectancy is concerned, I really need to take a leaf out of my grans' books. I was lucky to be in my forties and still have both grans alive. Sadly though, both passed away within six months of each other during the writing of this book – although I don't think there was any connection. Is it possible to die of embarrassment? Both my grans were soooooo different! One gran used to sit in the same chair day in, day out watching daytime TV. She'd sat in the chair for so long, it was dented in a perfect impression of her. Her special chair was off limits to everyone whenever anyone visited – no exceptions, not even the Queen. Mind you, I'd be surprised if anyone would have wanted to sit in it as it smelled of biscuits and wee. As for my other gran, well… She was known as the *village bike* where she lived as she was the *communal ride*. Bike-Gran was full of life despite her eighty-seven years. She dated men just to get into their wills. This is no joke – it was actual strategy she spoke about. Sometimes she would rage about it when it didn't work out. She was fuming with one of her last boyfriends since he only left her a Casio keyboard from Argos; my gran looked it up and it was on sale for £49.99. When she grumbled about him, she was pretty disappointed that she was left so little in his will as she'd apparently even given him a hand job. Bike-gran was even cracking jokes on her death bed. She chuckled that she was going to be buried on top of my grandad, who had died thirty-odd years previously, as he'd apparently never liked her on top! Given the choice of growing old, and how to act and behave, I think I know which gran's book I would choose to learn from!

But I can't lay all the blame on bad luck. I have spent a lot of my adult life prioritising work – my choice – but it wasn't necessarily a conscious one. I used to work in radio, and I loved it. It was a sociable job, and I have many friends still that I made in the studio or at promotional events. But I knew I was never going to get rich working in radio, so I left and set up my own cleaning company. I still run a cleaning company to this day. I also rent out houses. So, I know I have been very lucky; well, who am I trying to kid? I have worked bloody hard. I'm not good at many things in life, however, I can normally turn one quid into two by my opportunist ways.

I was so money obsessed when I was younger. Someone once told me everybody works for money, however, to make real money you have to make money work for you – well, I took on board this principle early on in life, buying houses, renting those houses – hence someone else is paying the mortgage for you. I used to be a bit of a Del Boy buying and selling stuff at auction to great success. I remember once buying loads of celebrities' autographs and as soon as one of them had died I used to sell them. David Bowie was a classic example of this; bought his autograph around 30-odd quid when he was alive, just after he died and listed on an online auction site, and it sold for almost ten times what I paid for it… Funny thing is, loads of David Bowie fans gave me so much abuse for cashing in on his death out of a mark of respect – I did leave it over two hours after his death before I listed it, I just replied to each of them saying it was too emotional to hang onto but anyway, it leaves me in a different position to most people I know. My friends are paying off mortgages, worrying about pensions and trying to create economic stability while raising a young family, whereas I am now able to retire early, but I haven't got any mini-mes to grow or anyone to share this with. So, I would have to admit my workaholic nature is probably my biggest downfall as to why I haven't settled down and got married.

But I realise now, work should not be just about

money; you have got to enjoy what you are doing as work takes up so much of life. The Dalai Lama once said, "We sacrifice our health to get wealth, then we sacrifice our wealth in order to get our health back." This is so true; you often find those who battle the daily grind in a job they hate can also be unhappy in their personal life too. My friends who have their own families and kids seem to think I have it all: a nice house, money, single and no responsibilities; however, I would swap pretty much everything to have a family of my own like they do.

And now I feel like my time is running out. It's not uncommon to hear about how women feel the clock ticking as they approach 40; I have female friends who talk about the pressure they are under to have babies – even when they don't want to! Did you imagine blokes feel this too? Many of us want families too and feel the pressure of time to make it happen. It's true, society might not hound us with it, but that also means we don't get to talk about it as much. Ruddy Hell! I don't think I can leave it much longer before I breed… In a few years' time, I'll struggle to raise a smile let alone anything else – plus, I can just imagine sports day with my child. At the rate I'm going, I'll be doing the egg and spoon race in a mobility scooter! Although, I heard a story a while ago from a friend of a friend that one of their kids was in the same class as Mo Farrah's kid; good luck with that one on sports day in the parents' race!!

But there's a chance all this worrying has got to me, and that recently I have been going through a mini mid-life crisis. I say mini; it could be full sized – but saying mini makes me feel at least a little in control. As I will tell you soon, I have found myself (deliberately) booking into a male MOT clinic and filling is an organ donation form. One thing is for sure, they won't want my funny eye – however, my penis hasn't had a lot of action recently, so perhaps that'll be good as new and ready for a new owner. It wouldn't be the weirdest donation ever; an entrepreneur in Brazil recently made national news as he dug a massive hole in the ground and was going to bury his expensive sports car. It turns out it was a publicity stunt to highlight the stupidity of humans burying such valuable things, like organs, when we can make a difference to someone else's life. Food for thought; and a penis ready for a new host.

I know that love comes in all shapes and sizes and can hit you at any time of life. We might not consider it very often, but even old people are looking for love – however, I'm not sure my gran was looking for the same kind of love as me. I once heard a heart-warming story about a bloke called Dave who was 82 and single. Proactive and energetic, he tried the personal ads in his local paper, however he didn't get much joy there. Then, he placed an advert in his friend's shop window looking for a 'companion'. All the national news agencies picked up on the story and a local radio station found him a lady. Flip me! What a result for them both! If I put an advert in a local shop window. I bet someone would offer me a golden retriever! (To be fair, those scrumptious pups make great companions though.)

But it is hard to stay pragmatic and hopeful. As I continue to date in my (increasingly) older years, it seems to me the longer you are single, the lower your standards tend to be. At first, I was looking for a model or a millionaire; I think these days if a lady's got a hole and can breathe, she will do… Joking aside, I wouldn't say I have got to the desperate stage just yet. I am, however, toying with the idea of shaving one of my legs, so when I'm in bed alone it will feel like I'm there with a lady!

Sooooo, I'm not a paragon of relationship perfection; I can't Marie Kondo your love life. In many ways, I'm still baffled by the chaotic nature of finding love. But that's exactly why you should read my book. As an average man, my lessons are your lessons. I'm not going to spit Pinterest memes at you and tell you if you work hard it will all work out. The evidence shows that clearly isn't true. It works out for around half of us. So, these days, you have similar odds of finding true love as you do of developing cancer. What I can do is help you to avoid the pitfalls and make the best of the positives while dating; I can help you feel like you're not the only one (you're not – you're part of about 50% of the population) and I can help you laugh at the bonkers world that is online dating. But I can't make love fair. After all, what kind of irony is it that makes it easier to pick up women when you are in a relationship? Apparently, once in a relationship you don't give off an air of desperation, so you're more attractive. That's just one of the many paradoxes that surrounds love.

And then, there's always the craziness of the most unlikely love stories. Crikey! Oscar Pistorius apparently found love when he was on house arrest so couldn't go out. He'd been charged with murdering his girlfriend AND he's got a missing leg!

Take from that what you can... I guess the first thing to take is that you don't need legs to be happy!

But, getting back to the point, let me summarise my romantic history to date so we can move on. What are my expert credentials? I have had four serious relationships and none of these began online. I have had two fingers up my bum (not at the same time); one and a half one-night stands (more about the half later); and I have even planned what I want on my headstone when I die. All this experience is punctuated with a whole list of online dating disasters along the way!

And I'm very pleased to meet all of you too!

The Place

I think it's important to know about my life to give context. After all, how can you trust me if you don't know me? And how can you understand my problems if you have no idea about where I live? I'm pretty certain the problems in finding love are different in London to Royston Vasey... Not that one is harder, but they certainly throw up very different obstacles to meeting new people.

I live in the real-life Royston Vasey. I grew up in a special place; it is a small town in Devon and it's unique. It has a population of 30,000 people, and yet as I mentioned earlier, it only has five different surnames. I think recently one more has been added, but it's just a rumour. Let's just say if there was a perfume ever named after this place it would be a called 'A Whiff of Incest'. Locally, it's also known as the graveyard of ambition and the main aim of girls when they leave school is to get pregnant and get social housing. The main aim of boys is to shag the prettiest girls. It's a simple place. It might sound like a stereotype, but stereotypes were born somewhere.

By my age, pretty much all the good-looking ladies have been *taken* and the ones who are still available would be a good subject matter for a reality TV series. It's fair to say if you are ever in a nightclub in my town at closing time when they turn the lights on, there is reason why these girls haven't pulled. An image of how I'd imagine Chernobyl survivors to look springs to mind!

My town has many pubs and a couple of clubs which might not stand comparison with the glitzy hipster bars and clubs of London. I once went in a bar in Shoreditch which was made up of small rooms each connected by wardrobe doors – it was a literal Narnia. In my town, clubs are dimly lit rooms with sticky carpets and it's not uncommon to hear the Cha-Cha Slide at some point in the evening. There used to be a brothel but it went out of business, believe it or not. That's the impact of the Credit Crunch for you. We used to share a joke locally that if you bought a girl a WKD blue on a night out you'd have her for life.

Sadly, that never really worked for me – and I did buy a few WKDs over the years.

We also once had a night club called 'Slappers'; yes, someone actually thought that was a great name. In fairness, it did live up to its moniker – I only went there once, but as I handed out the WKD blues, I got slapped by a girl. Anyway…

I guess every town has good and bad points, and despite my mocking, I love the place. It is home for me, and always has been, even when I have lived elsewhere. Everybody knows everybody, so there's never any privacy. But it is this care in the community spirit that brings everyone together. It is certainly full of characters, that's for sure, and I will introduce a few of them throughout this book. And, like every town, you also have the people who have given up on life who go and sit in the Wetherspoons all day long. Writing this book was my way of avoiding that fate. Although the WIFI in there is pretty good, and the free coffee refills are always tempting…

To help you imagine my town a little more clearly, I'll introduce you to some of the characters who everyone knows. Perhaps the first character I should describe for you is 'Funeral-Crasher' (I'm not going to give names, after all). He's come to be known for going to everybody's funerals in town whether he knew the person or not. He always sits at the back of the church crying his eyes out. Cynically, I swear he only goes to get the free buffet at the wake.

If you think this is strange behaviour, I have heard of worse. I once heard about a bloke who lived in Bridgwater – which is a town not too far away that people think is the twin of my hometown – who walks up and down the streets pretending to be a lorry. It would be funnier, only he apparently got sectioned a while ago as he tried to fuel up at the local garage by putting the pump in his pocket!

It's worth pausing on Bridgwater since I spent some of my early years working there – I knew my life had hit rock bottom when I was the chief baked bean stacker in charge of the night crew at a supermarket which at the time was called Safeway's. Anyway, one of my colleagues was a lady whose bits were back to front; by that I mean her fanny was located were her bum should have been. I shouldn't laugh as it was a birth defect, however she often made light of her plight. But she used to wear extremely tight leggings at night-time. There's no point beating around the bush – pun intended – you have all heard of the camel-toe, well, this was more like camel hoof! Moving on…

Another character stands out in my childhood memories. Many moons ago, way back in the 80s, my friend's dad used to run a pub. Like many places, it was subsequently shut down and has been turned into flats. After you read this, you might think it's a good job it was shut down! But I don't think the two incidents are related. This man has sadly passed away now, however he used to share so many stories, and some of them I have included in this book. One thing he didn't agree with was one-night stands and people cheating on their partners; he ranted about this frequently. Back in the 80s, he was responsible for filling up the condom machines in the gents' toilets in his pub. He felt it was his moral duty to challenge people on their philandering ways. So, while loading up the machines, he would put pin pricks into the condoms. God knows how many unwanted pregnancies he caused – let's just say he had a warped sense of humour…

Another story he once shared was when these two lesbians wanted to have a baby, this was back in the 80's when IVF wasn't that common. They persuaded to convince a regular at the pub to have sex with one of the lesbians in order to get her pregnant, cut a long story short. Six months he was having sex with her but she didn't get pregnant!! He failed to mention to her that he had already had the snip!!!!

Me and my people

The world is full of nut jobs; however, I would like to think I'm a pretty normal guy... (I have heard if you say something ten times you start to believe it, so I might repeat that bit a lot.) Put it this way, I have never stuck 26 Quality Streets up my bum and gone to A&E to have them removed – which is one story I heard one Christmas and have never forgotten. I'm not sure if the patient in question kept the wrappers on or not. I mean, I have heard of everyone hiding their favourite ones, but surely this is taking hiding too far! Personally, I love the purple ones the best, but I'm guessing he must have been hiding the long, gold fingers as I can't see you getting 26 of the green triangles up there, that's for sure!

Like dark chocolate and milk chocolate, my two brothers are completely different. Both of them have settled down and married, and they both have kids; one of them has more than he knows of – this is no word of a lie – I have been walking through the streets of my town before and had kids come up and say, "You're my Uncle Matt, aren't you?"

I didn't have a frigging clue who they were! Some family gatherings these days are like a refugee camp! Thankfully, I have never had any kids come up to me calling me 'Dad' and asking for pocket money!

Trying to be helpful, my eldest brother once advised when I meet the right lady I will *just know*.

Well, so much for that theory since his first marriage only lasted ten years. The strange thing is both my brothers ask me for relationship advice, yet I am the single one. But then, you often find that: people in relationships often turn to a single friend when they're in a crisis. Maybe I'm the only one who can come out?

In many respects, I've been lucky with my family. Being a middle child, I didn't suffer from any kind of middle child syndrome. However, I have heard it said that birth order affects your IQ. Apparently, first-borns are the smartest siblings because parents give them more undivided attention and encourage them to focus at school; whereas further down the sibling line, time gets compromised and parental overprotection lessens as they realise the kids stay alive even with a few germs. But this rule doesn't work out with my family; my youngest brother, John, excelled and was the most academic of the three of us. Mark and I were as thick as shit. To be fair, I think Mark probably was the thickest of us all and he was the eldest. Once at school, he was given a sheet of paper with different shapes on. There was a square, a circle and a triangle. There were no unusual shapes to trip him up. All he had to do was name the shapes for his homework – and he named the shapes after the three of us!

As children, we were lookers, as our neighbours all agreed. There aren't enormous amounts of photos to verify our handsomeness, but I trust Linda from next door; she's been eyeing us up since we were in our teens. In our heyday, we used to be in a church boyband. You have probably heard of the Bee-Gees; no, we didn't sound like them – even before our voices broke. Our surname is Bird, so we became known as the Bird-Gees. Nobody else could sing 'Kumbaya My Lord' like we could; in Devonian, it's pronounced *Kum-bye-arrr Me Lorrd,* of course. And we nailed the actions to 'He's got the whole world in his hands'. Some might argue this ruined our street credibility with the girls when we were younger, however we had fans. They were 82-year-old women who were probably stone deaf anyway. To be fair, most of the places we performed were like God's waiting rooms, with our audience made up of people just ready to pass over to the next life, and our tunes perhaps egging them on. Funnily enough, we recently discussed doing a 30-year reunion. Well, the idea was to be more of a tribute act to the Black-Eyed Peas. I'm sure you can see where this is going – we thought we'd call ourselves the Bird's-Eye Peas.

It's safe to say education wasn't for me. I was in the class of kids who dribbled and grunted; consistently in the bottom set for most things, I guess we were classed as retards back then. It might not be politically correct to call people that, but that's how school felt. Funnily, it wasn't the last time I've been judged or underestimated either. It wasn't all bad though; morning registration was always a laugh as I was the only coherent one. I'd joke around and have everyone in stitches. Laughter made being seen as bottom of the pack bearable; not that we were bottom of the pack – despite the grunting.

Funny enough, it was being in this class that meant I ended up being a cleaner. One school day, our year group were due to do some orienteering and the pupils were allowed outside the school grounds with maps and compasses. However, the teachers didn't trust our special class to leave the school grounds, so they gave us bibs and we had to go litter picking instead. It seemed a bit brutal at the time, but it set in motion a skillset that I have used to great success since.

I left school with an A in music and common sense; all the rest of my GCSEs were Es and Fs. It wasn't a terrible disaster though: I told my parents the grades were based on the alphabet with Z being the lowest, so they were incredibly proud of me. With this amazing success in the bag, they were subsequently a little surprised when I chose to leave school and work in a supermarket stacking shelves instead of going to Oxford or Cambridge!

When I turned 40, I went to a school reunion – it's funny to see how everybody has turned out. One piece of advice I would give my kids, if and when I have them, is to get with the ugly kids at school. All the good-looking girls from back in the day now look like swamp donkeys! Christ! One large lady made me laugh as she refused to eat any cake on offer. "Oh, I avoid things that make me fat," she said. I thought what like, "Scales, photographs and mirrors!" Yet all the ugly girls from school grew into beautiful women who are interesting. Plus, it just amazes me how people change and what paths they chose in life.

Re-meeting everyone invoked an immediately familiarity. In school, we all had nicknames, and it's funny how these names still stick well into adult life and came back to us in an instant. For example, one bloke I know was called Adrian and had the totally original nickname of Curly. This was for the completely unpredictable reason that when he was younger he had big curly hair like the Jackson Five. Now, he is in his fifties and bald, but he is still known as Curly.

Curly is a harmless nickname, but kids can be cruel. I remember a girl who used to put tissue in her bra at school, and we all called her Tissue-Tits. There was another girl who smelt of wee so we called her Pissy-Pants. Horribly, there was also a spotty girl we nicknamed Pizza-Face. Another was known as Gobble – get your minds out of the gutter – she had a body shaped like a turkey. I was known as Doey after the dodo bird since my surname is Bird. We really had the best imagination for names. Doey never stuck, but I have been called a number of things since then!

The funniest nickname I've heard was for a guy called Mark who everyone called Dyno-Rod. Poor chap! Apparently, he once had a problem weeing because his pee hole kept getting blocked. To solve this unfortunate issue, the doctor had to stick a rod down the centre of his shaft and twist it. The aim was for some hooks to be released which then scraped the inside of his penis to clear the blockage. God! I still cringe now when I see him! What a reminder! Perhaps adults are no kinder than kids! The last name I remember was for a kid we called Button Bollocks. This was for two reasons: once, he got a button stuck up his nose during a lesson and couldn't get it out; then a few days later, he got out of the shower, slid down the bannister rail naked and ripped his ball bag open... Still, it could have been worse!

I also know a guy who got his nickname after he went fishing as a kid with his friend. It was meant to be a fun day out, and they'd both been fishing before, so what could go wrong? Anyway, his mate cast the rod, and as he did, the hook caught in his eye and ended up taking his eye out completely! I've heard of fishermen having a third eye nowadays since they now have cameras that tell you where the fish are, but I don't think this boy's eye on a hook was an early invention of that. But it all worked out fine; he had a glass eye and he was given the original nickname of Hook-Eye.

But I digress – back to the reunion. Sometimes when you meet people from your past you can find yourself lost for words. It's not uncommon for people to lie by saying things like, '*You look well,*' or, '*You haven't changed a bit.*' I wasn't left with this option when I got into a conversation with one girl with whom I'd gone to school. She was now as fat as a house; she had the short and wide dimensions of a bungalow. I asked her how she was doing in life, and she said she had five kids with five different men. My first thought was Fathers' Day must be confusing. But she continued listing her family; it turns out she is also a granny and just going through another divorce. This set up a stark comparison since I have not done any breeding yet, and it's currently on my next-steps plan. But I did lie slightly: I told her I was sorry to hear she was getting divorced again, but in my head I was thinking, *Ruddy hell! I bet she's probably eaten him!*

While I was busy judging Bungalow-Girl, I didn't notice my own judgement coming to call. I bumped into a former teacher and she asked what I did for a job. I told her I was a cleaner. She tilted her head to one side, gave me her best sympathy look and said, "Well, it's a job isn't it?" Being on the receiving end of judgement sucks! But I didn't like to say, *'Well, actually, I'm the director of the company and own nine houses.'* Life isn't about how much you have; it's more about who you have. In reality, I have a lot to thank this teacher for as whenever I did any work at school, she would always say the same thing: "You have done well, but you could do better." Her philosophy has inspired me since. I believe the minute you *think* you have achieved something, you stop achieving.

Have you ever noticed how you always tend to bump into people when you least expect to or when you are not looking your best? I've been judged many other times over the years as people make their minds up about me on a small amount of information. I spent many years as a toilet cleaner, and this I have found is typically a game changer when you are asked by a date what you do for a living. Friends have told me to *big* myself up a little and describe myself as a janitor instead. Apparently, it sounds so much sexier than a toilet cleaner.

I remember one specific moment where I felt the wrath of a woman's prejudice, and it was the moment I realised that there are women who would refuse to date a man because of his employment alone. A few years ago, I was cleaning a toilet in a small village, and as I walked out of the public convenience I bumped into a stunning girl. She took one look at me, admittedly I was holding a bog brush, and she turned away. I went to say hello but her face just screamed at me in silence: *Please don't let this toilet man talk to me.* That was the moment; I knew some girls will always look down on you for your career choice. But then, I guess these girls are the ones to best avoid. On a connected note, it's funny when doing online dating how many more messages you get when you change your job description from cleaner to company director.

I have enjoyed a varied work life. After leaving school with almost no qualifications, I had an ambition of one day working in radio. Firstly, as I have already mentioned, I worked in supermarkets until the age of 21. Then one day on the way to work, I heard an advert on the radio for a station in Bristol who were looking for promotional staff to be the face of the station. At the time I thought I was a bit of a looker, but I probably wasn't really. However, that wasn't going to stop me – thankfully, I was also a bit cheeky. I got an interview, and headed to Bristol.

So, there I was in a room of 50 people, feeling excited. One of the tasks was to stand on a table and sell yourself to the rest of the group. All the cool kids were standing up, cocking eyebrows and adopting a swagger, saying, "Hi! I'm Gary. I love to skateboard in my spare time *blah blah blah*." I wasn't cool so I wasn't about to brag about my surfing skills, or how I could break dance because, believe me, I can't – whenever I hit the dancefloor I look like I'm having a fit! St John's Ambulance need to be on stand-by when I bust some moves. Anyway, where was I? Oh – back then, I had been writing lots of poetry, and I could remember some of it off by heart. When it came to my turn, I stood up and climbed onto the table. The room went silent. I took a breath and smiled at the room. And then I began to recite my poem. It was called 'Painful Poo', and it is about that moment we have all experienced. You know, when you go squeeze but nothing comes out. Here is a small snippet of it:

Painful Poo
Painful Poo is bad I know
Especially when you want to, but you just can't go
It is as though the poo is playing a game on your bum,
Like waiting at the station and the train don't come
You grit your teeth, prise your cheeks apart
But all that comes out is a blurping fart.
You check the pan to see what you have done
But nothing has come out your bleeding bum.
You look around the bathroom to take your mind off things
The poo enters the departure lounge, and the ruddy telephone rings
After debating whether to answer the phone or not
Out it comes in one big lot
Little logs, big logs, all different shapes too
It's amazing when you think about the different types of poo.

Well, that little gem of a poem got me a job in radio. I was always told that in an interview you needed to stand out from the crowd, and I guess a bit of constipation humour was enough to be remembered. Perhaps it goes to show any attention is good attention…

I then spent the next 12 years making jingles and commercials for different stations. I also did the odd bit or presenting as well as promotion work, which was kind of strange as I don't really have the voice for it. I sound like a special farmer! Regardless of my suitability, I loved it! The carnivals, the early mornings, the gigs and sticker spots. All of it. From producing shows to being on air, no two days were ever the same. But, it's true what they say in life – the jobs you love the most often pay the least.

And that journey started with my little poem. Feel free to use it yourself in a job interview. You might also find it lucky!

I love to laugh; it's been so important to me over the years; from helping me to survive school to getting me jobs, laughter has been my medicine and my joy. I also believe laughter is soooo important in a relationship. It galvanises your relationship and helps you through the bad times. My longest relationship lasted nine years, and I put our success (we're still friends) down to our shared laughter. I met her in a petrol station of all places. She was my Lego lady: we connected straight away and even though we ended up more like siblings, we spent most of the relationship laughing and play-fighting. Once, she threw her dirty pants at my head, and when they missed, they stuck to the hotel wall! I called her Pritt-Stick Pants after that moment. We were just so comfortable with each other; probably too comfortable. We had this one occasion where she weed on me when she was drunk; I'm not sure I ever fully recovered from that one. I was lying next to her at the time when I suddenly felt this warm, wet feeling against my leg – it was too late to move; she was out cold, blissfully unaware. I just lay there thinking, *My girlfriend has weed on me.*

There is another thing I don't miss from that relationship – she had a wind problem. Plus, she would find it funny, pushing one out and trying to force my head under the covers to smell it. She called them Love Puffs, and said it was a sign of showing her affection. I still say it wasn't pleasant! I don't want affection in fart form. I told her she should go and assist the US military to find Bin Laden. When the press published the rumours he was hidden in caves in Afghanistan, I suggested sending her in and she would soon smoke him out! I mean, there was no need for that sort of behaviour in the bedroom – it was nearly as bad when I was young and my mum would lick her hanky to then clean a mark or snot from my face. God, I hated when she did that. And, then there's the time when Pritt-Stick Pants shit herself. I was casually watching TV when she came running in from work and jumped straight into the bathtub. There was diarrhoea literally dripping from her clothes – I hosed her down with the shower while she was fully clothed – if that's not a sign of love, I don't know what is. And some people still question whether I loved her!

Pritt-Stick Pants and I even shared an amusing break-up. On Valentine's Day, we went to see a romantic movie together at the cinema. It was called 'He's Just Not That Into You', and the reviews had been relatively good for a rom-com movie. But on the way out, it raised so many questions about us we decided to go our separate ways. We have stayed in touch though; she has moved on and is now happily married with kids. It's lovely to see she has found her happy ending.

It might be strange, but I am still in touch with all my serious past relationships; well, all except for one lady, The Ex. Isn't it a truth that it is too hard to stay in touch with the one who hurts you the most?

This one lady, The Ex as she is referred to in this book, was a widow who I dated for about four years. I was 36 at the time we got together, which would have been prime breeding age for me, but she was about five years older and already had two kids. To her credit, she was upfront and honest and said she didn't want any more, and at the time, I was okay with that. I guess she is the closest I have ever come to being married and I honestly felt like I could grow old with her. For the first time, I felt like I had a purpose in life. She changed my whole outlook; she gave me the attitude I mentioned, that it is not about what you have but the people you have around you. She helped me to see you must always remember to live for today, and not just prepare for the future.

Looking after her children was the closest I have come to being a dad too. The kids were aged ten and six at the time I got together with their mum. Even though they were not my children, I really loved them and considered us to be a family. One of the best moments in my life was when the six-year-old girl turned around one day and said, "I really wish you were my dad." She had only been two when her dad sadly passed away with a brain tumour so she didn't remember him. Those words meant so much to me.

I confess that I felt like a complete failure for this relationship not working out. I think the saddest part was knowing if her husband was still alive, they would have stayed married for life. Sometimes in life you can try your best, but your best is just not good enough. But still, you learn something from every relationship you are in, and among the things I mentioned above, and the many other lessons, I guess she also taught me to not be so judgmental too. On paper, we should never have got together. If you had told me many years ago I would settle down with a lady with two kids, who lived on benefits and smoked occasionally, I would have laughed at you. However, it's very easy to judge someone without knowing them.

After that relationship breakdown I took time out from the world of love. I think it shows a complete lack of respect to jump from one relationship to the next. Besides, I was in too much pain for some time. It was after about a year of being single I felt emotionally ready to meet someone again. A sad thing is, I have friends who can't be single; they need to be in a relationship. I guess I've been lucky that I have never felt the need to be with someone, even in my loneliest moments.

Once the year was up, I realised how much harder it was getting to meet someone. Nowadays, my generation don't really go out to nightclubs. Hence, we have embraced online dating. You'd think with so many of us online, dating would be easy. But it's not. Not only do people judge me because of my job, but women also react to my relationship CV. I really thought that my lack of divorce or children would appeal to the ladies – I thought past *baggage* was a hindrance. How wrong I was! So many ladies question why I have never settled down and why I don't have kids. It's like I might be some kind of weirdo. And this reminds me of a question I have always wanted to ask: did Father Christmas have any kids of his own?

I fondly remember dating when we were basically still kids. The dating game was brutal, naturally, but we didn't have all this modern tech stuff, dating apps and Photoshop. I think the only stress we had back then was playing football in the street and the ball getting stuck under a car or playing Kirby and the ball going into the neighbour-from-Hell's garden. Ah! How simple it all was! It's crazy to think about how much stress we bring into our lives these days. And yet, we create pretty much all of it ourselves: work stress, relationship stress, home stress... I try not to take life too seriously. Even the smallest things can drag you down.

But some worries are unavoidable, and there are a few that get through to me. Just recently, I had another life-changing moment. Moving into my 42nd year, I thought it would be a good idea to have a male fertility MOT. Some people might think this was weird, however, I thought about it long and hard – no pun intended. My theory behind it was if I did have a low sperm count, I could possibly freeze them, or if I was firing blanks I could just forget about this whole finding a breeding partner idea and start to move on altogether.

So, I phoned a private clinic in Bristol. My initial plan was to do a sample at home and drop to them. However, I lived in Taunton at the time, and the receptionist said I needed to get my specimen to them within the hour. I thought, *Blimey! That might be pushing it!* With both the receptionist and I realising the logistical issue, I suggested, "What about if I stopped at Bridgwater services and bashed one out? I could definitely make it in time!"

The receptionist did NOT see the funny side at all! Instead, she advised it was best I came to (or should I say *at?*) the lab. So, I enquired how much this service was, and she explained it was £110 pounds. I thought, *Flip me! This is going to be the most expensive tug ever!* Plus, they don't even lend a hand within this price!

Booking made and paid for, she chose this moment to tell me I was not allowed to masturbate for a couple of days prior to giving a sample. A COUPLE OF DAYS! My mind exploded! *Well, Christ!* I thought. *I'm a single bloke! How am I going to cope?* I was certain that Bob Geldof, on hearing of my plight, would do a charity record to help me recover from the trauma of lack of tugging!

Anyway, the appointment was booked for 11am. And I certainly walked into the clinic a lot differently to how I walked out (and I'm not just referring to the tension in my balls). When I arrived, I was the only person in the waiting room; I didn't know what to expect, or whether all the *tossers* would be called in one by one. I gave my name at the counter and was told to take a seat.

A nurse called out my name and gave me a sample pot and a questionnaire to fill in, and showed me to my room. I thought it was probably best to do the form first and get it over and done with before I made myself *comfortable*. There was no point rushing things; it was a day out after all! Although, it was not quite the same as a picnic with friends or a trip to the zoo. At least, after the few days of tugging-ban, there was no fear of getting stage fright, that's for sure!

So, I followed the nurse and entered the private, little room. It was all white with just a seat, a TV, a set of headphones and a pile of magazines. I looked around, and finished the form, and then began to make myself comfortable. Putting the headphones on, I then got to watch some porn. But after three minutes the movie stopped and a sign appeared across the screen – to watch more I had to pay three quid on a credit card. I thought, *Ruddy hell! You'd expect more after paying £110 for this experience!* I then thought, *Stuff this!* So, I turned the DVD off and back on again, and I watched the intro again for another three minutes. I thought I might as well get my money's worth!

After 30 minutes and several loops of the intro, my mission was complete. I had filled the pot up! I'm surprised Muller hadn't tried to contact me as there was enough to fill a yoghurt pot. I put my clothes back on and rang the doorbell next to a hatch where I had to hand the sample over. A middle age women poked her head through, and the first thing she said to me was, "How was that for you?"

Taken aback, I replied, "Pardon?" as I handed her my pot of spunk.

I was rather embarrassed when she repeated exactly the same: "How was that for you?"

I replied the only thing I could think of: "It was okay, thank you." I'm still not sure why I thanked her. Feeling awkward, I tried to make a quick escape, but she continued, "Let me check we have all your details…"

And, get this! They need the sample to be fresh – they must have it within an hour of ejaculation. However, the results take two weeks to come through!

During this personal crisis, I found out a few things about masturbation that I didn't know. I learned tugging has health benefits. It is actually good for you! Did you know you reduce your risk of prostate cancer by having more orgasms? It's true I'm no scientist – you've heard about my GCSE results – however, it is all to do with flushing out harmful toxins when you ejaculate. We definitely don't want anything harmful building up!

When I left my little room, the waiting area was full – I thought I'd taken too long so a queue was building up! But some things in life shouldn't be rushed, especially if you are paying £110. I wanted to enjoy the experience! I suppose it's like mixing up an Angel Delight: if you rush it, you don't get the right pudding. If you are patient and wait a little longer, it comes out perfect!

A great comparison!

When I told my mum about my little day trip to Bristol, and how much it cost, the first thing she said was, "They saw you coming." I genuinely hope they didn't, however I do have a pretty good sex face. She also dropped in, "It would have been cheaper to go to the zoo."

Anyway, I'm beginning to ramble. I'm coming to my final autobiographical notes, for a moment anyway. I have thought about how I want to be remembered when I die. God forbid it's not for years to come, but it helps me to make decisions as I live based on how I want to be remembered. I guess everyone wants to leave a legacy. I want people to remember that I didn't take things too seriously. We find so much more happiness in the lighter side of life.

Approaching my mid-40s now, I am at an age where some of my friends' parents are sadly dying. Death certainly puts everything into perspective, but even in the face of death we still need to stay positive. Some funerals I have attended recently have been quite comical – albeit by accident. But some humour does lighten the mood on such sad occasions. There was one occasion where the song chosen for when the coffin was leaving the church was supposed to be *Angels* by Robbie Williams. Accidentally, the technician pressed the wrong number on the CD player. Rather than a beautiful and mournful rendition of remembrance, everyone had 20 seconds of *Old Before I Die* blasted out around the church.

I don't want my death to be taken too seriously either. If I'm honest, I've been inspired by Spike Milligan; on his headstone, his final words boldly state: *I told you I was ill.* I think this is genius! So, when I'm dead and buried, I also want people to walk past my grave and smile. In my will, it is now stated that my headstone should say: *Here lies Matt Bird, stiff at last.*

Not that I have ever had a problem in that department.

INTRODUCTION

(The Formal Bit)

Are you, like 35% of the country, struggling to find love? Contrary to the feeling, you are most definitely not alone. The Office for National Statistics states that 35% of British adults are single. They also show the number of marriages has fallen, and still almost 50% of those that happen end in divorce. It appears as we have become more scientific, technological and *civilised*, we have become shitter at love.

But all is not lost! Thankfully for you, I have just finished a lengthy study into dating, and I focus on online dating in particular. For our mutual benefit – and for my sanity – I have reframed my countless disastrous dates as primary research into the possibilities and difficulties in finding love; there has to be some purpose to having so many drinks with so many nutjobs and swamp donkeys, surely? Subsequently, I have organised this gathered wisdom to help you onto the love-seeking pathway that seems to have become somewhat confused in modern times. I have begun to see meeting new people and dating as some kind of pirate hunt for treasure – just like Long John Silver seeking the elusive X marking the spot, finding love is a whole bunch of contradictions: it is both an adventure and a battle, exciting and an effort, romantic and to be carefully judged.

Ultimately, I hope my dating experiences can help us all to understand what the pursuit of love might be in the 21st century; though I can't promise we'll be any closer to knowing how to find the intangible Happily Ever After. That sadly remains as a pot of gold at the end of the rainbow. At least, I can eliminate some of the ways love can't be found, reducing the possibilities for failure. After all, you might not be that loveable and you might look like a swamp donkey. And anyway, I am still single (a plot spoiler, I know, but I'd hate to be accused of false advertising).

Firstly, let's dispel some myths, such as the assumption that less marriages means more of us are crap at love. Over the last 40 years, divorce rates have stayed more or less the same, at around 110,000 per year. These have fluctuated a bit, but in 2015 there were less divorces than in 1972. The reason the statistics appear so dramatic is that the number of marriages has fallen by almost 50% which changes the ratio from one divorce in four marriages to one in two. True, if there's fewer marriages but the same divorce rates then it seems obvious that more are failing. But the statistic does not take into consideration any other factors, such as how long couples have been married before divorcing, or how many people are serial-wedders. I mean, we have all heard of the seven-year itch, but flip me! Where I come from, people are scratching after a year of marriage. But then, that might be the lice... The most important statistic to note is that there are less marriages in a society that has increased in population by over 25%. Can this truly be equated to a breakdown in family units, failed relationships and a proclivity for romantic discontent? Or do we just engage differently with the tradition of weddings and marriages? Perhaps our increasingly secular beliefs deter people from the eternal knot-tying, or perhaps it's the fact the average wedding these days costs the same as a deposit on an equally unaffordable house? And we all know we can't have *everything* we want. Still, I've never been married, but I believe in the concept of it and I would love to walk that aisle one day. Although, they do say marriage is grand, but divorce normally costs thirty grand or more.

Within these statistics I gleaned from the ONS are lots of unanswered questions. For example, just how many of the marriages and divorces are experienced (Enjoyed? Suffered?) by serial brides and grooms? I mean, they do say the difference between love and marriage is that love is blind and marriage is an eye opener.

How many couples cohabit without getting married? How many of these remain stable? How many break up? Then there are the questions about marriages themselves: has the Credit Crunch impacted on our choice to marry? I heard of one couple from Bristol who held their wedding reception for 33 guests in McDonalds! Apparently, they love McNuggets and milkshakes, but I think the £150 bill must have had something to do with it.

Has social media upped the pressure on weddings conforming to ever increasing demands for style and aesthetics? And if so, has that impacted on whether a wedding is even possible or desirable? Are there people out there waiting to be able to have the wedding of their dreams, and would rather have no wedding at all than compromise? Have our increasingly secular lifestyles decreased the value of marriage as an institution? The answers to these questions, and many more, might shed new light on why so many of us haven't married outside of outdated social expectations that leave us feeling like failures. Instead of spotlighting inadequacy and difference, exploring these questions might provide a kaleidoscope of experiences; love might be just one chunk of our fruitful and fulfilled lives rather than the measure of the whole pie. And we should get to choose the fillings we want. Mind you, I'm sure I've been on several dates with some of Mr Kipling's daughters – they were certainly exceeding!

But I digress. This is not a book about marriage; it is a book about dating. Like Jane Austen and Helen Fielding, and all the great romance writers before me, I am writing about the pursuit of love – the pursuit of potential marriage. However, while they write about courting, romance, and suitable partners, I am writing about how to make the initial connection. And from a man's point of view. I don't think there's enough of men's voices in this genre. Lots of people assume men don't care as much about romance or marriage, but it's not true. I definitely feel my biological clock ticking. I might not have the same biological barriers as women, but I still have societal expectations. A man's point of view might be crass or ugly at times, but I am handing the inner workings of the male mind to you on a plate. Well, on paper anyway.

In the usefully organised chapters ahead, I explore dating in the 21st century. Through my experiences, I reveal my expectations of romance and dating, exposing the ridiculous and flawed ways in which they work on my esteem and sense of value. I describe both good and bad dates, awkward moments, and try to get to the heart of why I haven't found my life-long love yet. I have been open-minded and dated people I wouldn't normally meet, discovering we can't help who we're attracted to. But the biggest problem I have is that most of the women I have met weren't who they said they were. If women are having the same problem, online dating is flawed before we even get in the first drink.

People argue finding love is hard, but in theory it should be easier than ever before. With social media and the de-stigmatisation of organised dating opportunities, love has been marketised and globalised. But somehow we don't seem to be finding the connections for which we all yearn. I did some maths on eHarmony – one of the biggest sites that's reportedly also one of the most successful. It's a paid site too, with almost one million members forking out anywhere up to £44 per month to access all features. But there are around 10 million UK-based users, and on its home page, eHarmony report users finding love every 14 minutes. That's a mere 35,040 every year.

That means around 0.03% chance of finding a partner.

That's not good odds.

I guess if it was too successful, it would quickly run out of customers.

And I suppose that therein lies the problem, as tragic as that may be.

So, this book is my contribution to the conversation about finding lurve; at the end of the day, love is not a crime, and you can't help who or what you fall in love with. Mind you, I'm not sure I condone the marriage of a bloke in Venezuela who married his horse! I believe that is wrong on soooo many levels! But I believe we should challenge these monolithic giants, the enormous dating websites, who purport to offer the key to lasting relationships, but really are less ethically taking your money than gyms in January.

So, I hope you enjoy my stories – at least far more than I have any way! And, whether you find your One or you become a cat person, or focus on your career, or raise a family alone, or travel: whatever love story you write, love it!

LOVE IN THE NATURAL

WORLD

Or how channelling our inner

Attenborough can help us find love

Over my four-plus decades, I have been lucky enough to meet some amazing people, and I have learned that everyone has a story to tell. This book is a new take on the oldest story of all – it is a tale as old as time: the story of finding love. As the title of this book suggests, I think finding true love online is as rare as seeing a baby pigeon. But that doesn't mean it's impossible. There is a saying about how finding love is like finding shoes – at first, people go for the good-looking, smart ones, but always end up with the ones they feel most comfortable with. I'm not sure if this is true in the animal kingdom, where some birds choreograph interesting dance routines with their buddies, and other beasts fight to the death. Animals show us there's a broad range of techniques. So, like a human-love-themed David Attenborough, I have chronicled my search. I will entertain you with tales of rutting seasons, the myriad of natural plumages, the variety of mating calls and the innovative evolution of human love rituals in the digital age.

Throughout, I refer regularly to my dad's advice. Let me remind you: he said, "Don't go looking for love; let love come to you." This advice has stayed with me as indelible and sage wisdom. But at the heart of this advice is an insecurity; what if love doesn't come to me? What does his advice mean anyway? We can't all be like my father or staircases would be simultaneously the most exciting and the most dangerous places in the UK! We'd find horny men and women lurking mid-case, jostling and bumping innocent passers-by. Perhaps that's how the rule of no passing on the stairs came about – it was to avoid any unnecessary canoodling. And what about how stairs have evolved; does that mean lifts and escalators are equally valid bumping places? If you're an escalator-traveller, your chances are immediately diminished by the fact ascenders and descenders are separated by an aisle. We'd have to wistfully watch as the person of our dreams escalates smoothly away in the opposite direction at a comfortable walking speed. It would be like an even more dull version of Sliding Doors – without the cheating as no couples will have ever met.

At points throughout this read, it might come across that I don't have a heart. You might not credit my own opinion on this matter – after all, how well could the Grinch recognise his own aortic deficiencies before his great epiphany? However, I can assure you my heart is of the correct and proper size. As evidence for my emotional sincerity, I once took in a wounded baby pigeon which I found in my garden. I nursed it back to health before releasing it back into the wild – I felt like a more manly Michaela Strachan and was proud of my zoological prowess. I realise it is a common perception that pigeons are dirty creatures that spread diseases; some might even go as far as to say they need to be eradicated. But on that spring day in my garden it was a bird in need, and I was faster than a pellet from an air rifle. It's true to say I have never taken advantage of a vulnerable bird before; I guess my religious upbringing imbued in me a strong belief in caring for those in need regardless of circumstance or species.

My big heart extends to my beloved pets as well. I have two cats: Smirnoff, who is a wise and handsome cat; and a deaf, ginger cat with down syndrome called Dave. Dave has not actually been medically diagnosed with DNS, however, I home-diagnosed him after his symptoms matched the list I found on Wikipedia. Plus, he grunts instead of purrs.

I have learnt so much from both my cats. For instance, Dave taught me soooo much about happiness; such as: however bad a deal life hands you, smile and get on with it. He is such a happy cat; if he had thumbs instead of paws, he would put them up to everyone who passed him. He reminded me of a lady I once knew with no legs as she was always smiling – which just goes to show you don't need legs to be happy. Mind you, she was in one of those motorised wheelchairs, so it might have been the G-force making her pasty-shaped smile as she whizzed past!

Dave is also deaf as a post; however, I once had a moment where I thought he could hear, and from that I learned how to talk to him. This story is so miraculous, you won't want to believe it, but I promise, it is a true story. It was a sunny day, and I was playing Bob Marley with the volume ramped up. The song had a strong, deep baseline and I swear I saw Dave shake his ass to the rhythm. He was busting out some cat-moves. Even his tail swished in time. Ever since then, whenever I need to call him in, such as for dinner, I use the deepest, lowest voice I can muster. It seems to work. I shout, "DAVE! DINNER TIME!" gurning out my best Barry White impression, and in the wobbles. I'm sure my neighbours must think I am a total nutjob, but I'm not sure it's any worse than the common baby-talk, coo-chi-woo, high-pitched voice I often hear used for small children and cute animals. Besides, doesn't everyone speak to their pets and have a specific voice for them?

As for Smirnoff, well, he is the love of my life. He is my four-legged, fur-covered soul-mate. We have lived together for 18 years, on and off. He has genuinely taught me the meaning of love. Our meet-cute moment, that moment when two individuals know they're meant for each other forever, happened a few years ago after a terrible incident. Smirnoff was in a car accident, and his head was knocked off. Don't worry – he wasn't driving! Weirdly (and you'll find out later just how weird) he got knocked over by a yellow metro. I'm fairly certain it wasn't the same yellow metro I lost my virginity in 20-odd years previously, though that would be some crazy-mad revenge if the two incidents were related. I'm sure you want to know more… but you'll have to wait till chapter eight to find out. Thankfully, a kindly bystander took him to the vets.

Smirnoff had been microchipped so they managed to contact me to inform me of the accident. The vet had stark news: "Look. We might not be able to save him. But we can try to put his head back on." He abruptly laid out my choices: "The operation will cost around £400 or you can buy a new cat for 20 quid."

Now, some people say I can be tight with my money, however, there was no choice that day: I instructed the vet to operate.

After the operation, I went in to visit Smirnoff. The vet warned me my cat probably wouldn't recognise me; Smirnoff wouldn't let anyone near him at that point. However, as soon as I peeked round the door, I looked at him and he looked at me. Our eyes met and there was an instant and powerful connection, like your phone automatically connecting to the WIFI when you get home. If cats could smile, he beamed. His little eyes squinted with joy and love. He was all over me. In that moment I knew the meaning of love – even if it did cost me 400 quid and a sleepless night to learn it.

My house was a strange place for a while after that; it felt like a care in the community home for cats. My work as a cat-dad was more important than ever, with Down-syndrome Dave walking around grunting and dribbling, and Smirnoff with his head hanging down on one side!

Aside from my love of my feline companions, I also share my home and my life with some grunters. I have recently purchased some piglets and plan is to breed them in a few months' time. I will obviously set the romantic scene; I will put some candles out in the sty, blast out a bit of Barry White (although I might have to choose a different playlist or Dave might be along for the ride). Hopefully, they will make sweet music... well, sweet oinking and rutting. Don't panic, they are not from the same town. You could call their marriage arranged as I carefully selected them. He is called Kevin Bacon, and since she has eyes like the Icelandic pop star Bjork, I named her Pjork. The arranged nature of their relationship hasn't been a hindrance so far, and they both love getting down and dirty in the mud and swill.

I'm convinced some of their behaviour could be considered piggy foreplay, as I have caught Kevin snorting around Pjork a few times. But I have some concerns that Kevin might have some special needs. I mean, just the other night I heard some proper squealing going on down at the sty, so I hope Kevin knows which hole to stick it in... I guess, like my first sexual experience, as you will find out later, it's all trial and error. As you know, education was lost on me. But really, don't get me started on the quality of my sex education; we might have been taught how to put a condom on a cucumber, but no one taught us where to stick the ruddy thing afterwards.

My love of and learning from wildlife doesn't end at cats, pigs or pigeons. It's important to be interested in nature as a lot of human sexual behaviours get named after the natural world. For example, did you know the term '*love rat*' stems from the fact there are more rats in England than humans, and that rats are not fussy where they stick it? If you are a rat in a sewer with your ass in the air, any other rat running past will see this as an open invitation. Although, I don't think rat sex is relegated to sewers; any street-side, warm kitchen, barn or loft area will do. They really aren't fussy and they really are horny. It is the same with rabbits, hence the phrase '*at it like rabbits*'. They are always breeding.

There are more correlations than mere colloquialisms too. Did you know there is a theory that the bigger the bird the more loyal they are? Take emus, for example, they mate for life. Similarly, swans stay with the same partners until death, and the surviving partner often lives alone when one dies prematurely. So maybe me attracting the larger bird might not be a bad thing after all! Saying that, on the other side of the bird spectrum, sparrows and blue-tits are in and out of the sexual health clinic on a regular basis. They are constantly ruffling feathers, and sweet-tweeting each other. They have to get their bird-bits checked due to their promiscuous sexual activity; they want their breadcrumbs and to eat them. With this in mind, perhaps being a fat-bird magnet is not such a bad thing after all! And finally, let's not forget peacocks and their beautiful feathers which they love to display; they love to flutter, preen and show off. As beguiling as this display is to us, in reality they're just trying to get laid.

Though we can learn a lot from animals, I often think it would be great if human mating rituals were as simple as those of the animal kingdom. I'd definitely benefit if finding a breeding partner was as easy as it is in the goat world. Traditional methods state that firstly you put a ram in a field neighbouring all the female goats for the best part of a week; I think this is to give the ram a chance to eye up all the ladies. Then after the week is done, you let the ram loose in the field with all the females. Apparently, the ram's first tactic is to go up to the female goats and kick them in the legs. If they don't run off, they are ripe for breeding. Apparently, this is called tupping! How simple would a night out be if you could just go up and kick a bird in the shins to find your breeding partner!

Though it's not all simplicity and tupping: I'm not sure I'd want to rut horns like a male stag to fight for a partner. Or a male rhino for that matter. And I certainly don't want to become dinner after a little rumpy-pumpy like male praying mantises who get eaten by the post-coitally peckish females.

I mean, some facts you hear about the animal kingdom are truly shocking. Ducks, for example, rape each other – and they don't use duck-tape either (I promise this is my worst pun – there has to be a worst one, doesn't there?) And I'll never forget the David Attenborough documentary where a dolphin tried to drown another dolphin by placing his dolphin-dick in the other one's blow hole!

I think it's safe to say many of nature's examples are best avoided.

Back to the internet then.

SECTION TWO:

WHAT I HAVE LEARNED

ABOUT LOVE SO FAR

Chapter 1: Lessons Learned

Or, how pain is a good teacher!

Lesson 1: Bitterness Equals Blindness

As always, there is a thin line between love and hate. But in truth, I could never hate that one ex; the one I thought was The One. I mean, *I could*, but I don't. Some days hatred *could* come naturally, but I *choose* not to. After all, I have learned from my parents that an eye for an eye will make the whole world go blind.

This is a belief I practice. And I do mean practice: if it was easy we wouldn't need a saying.

But it is easy to get bitter and twisted when a relationship breaks down. None of us are free from this truth; feeling bitterness can be as natural as breathing. Yes, even for me (and obviously, I am perfect). Everyone else's break ups always seem easier to suffer and much simpler to solve. I struggled for many reasons after my biggest break up, but especially after giving The Ex a generous financial settlement. Simply put, what some might deem fair another perceives as being ripped off. The reasons for either argument are irrelevant now. I'm more interested in focusing on the skill of not giving in to those negative, angry feelings. It can be even worse still when you can understand how both sides are true; like some kind of demented Schrödinger's Cat[1], I was tormented by knowing I was simultaneously the innocent victim and the twat. I could have justifiably been caught up in arguing over keeping what I had worked for; but we had chosen to share our lives for a time, and I had to accept responsibility for the fact I had chosen to share mine with her. Bitterness would just cost me twice.

---

[1] Schrödinger was an eminent physicist who has been made internationally famous by the sit-com 'The Big Bang Theory'. In simple terms, to prove how scientific theory works, Schrödinger stated that if you place a cat and something that could kill the cat in a box and sealed it, you would not know if the cat was dead or alive until you opened the box. So, until the box was opened, the cat was (in a sense) *both* dead AND alive. I'm brutally subverting Schrödinger's cleverness to say that two opposing facts can be true at the same time. I'm that clever. But you didn't need me to explain it because you are too. Obviously. (And I didn't need to look him up on Wikipedia to find out either.)

Therefore, as the famous Disney song says, I had to *Let It Go*! Bitterness in the present is more an enemy than any grudge from the past.

Lesson 2: Time is Precious

My time with The Ex wasn't all bad. Among other things, she taught me that time is precious. I'm a simple guy, so for me straight-forward sums can reveal a clear way of processing my emotional responses.

For example, there are 86,400 seconds in a day. If something goes wrong, often we only notice in short bursts of time. The bad moment might only be a couple of minutes, but this can negatively affect us for the rest of the day. This is true even when we cannot do anything about it. We can experience annoyance, frustration and anger for hours after a bad event which can cloud our judgement and appreciation of the many good things that happen too. After all, our days are often made up of both good and bad moments.

As a response, I learned to ask, why let 120 seconds spoil the other 86,280 seconds?

Lesson 3: Revenge is not payback; revenge is moving on!

The best revenge is to find love again. Looking for payback only creates pain for you again. As hard as it seems, turn your gaze to the future, and invest in the relationships that are in your present.

Life is far too short to spend it being vengeful and having hang-ups on past relationships.

Lesson 4: Great things can come out of tough times

After all the heartbreak, it turns out I have a lot to thank The Ex for. The happy moments we shared together, and the family life we built for a while, taught me a lesson I had missed while I was working: life is not about how much we have but about who you have.

Lesson 5: Money cannot buy you love

As someone who has always worked hard and assumed that hard work and success would bring love and happiness, I was particularly slow to learn this lesson. I know: I've already admitted to being a slow learner so this is no surprise. But it was a surprise to me! Sadly, I had to have my heart broken like a bear without honey to learn it.

And it was one of the most heart-breaking moments in my life – bar the separation from the woman whom I believed would be my life partner. It all began when my business had been booked to clean a women's refuge between Christmas and New Year's Eve. As you might be able to imagine, it is a difficult time of year to be in a refuge, seeking safety when the rest of the world appears to be indulging. It's such a funny time of year, and until this point, I'd never fully appreciated how much emotion and expectation we attach to this holiday. I've always been happy to work over the holidays, and I was always happy to miss out on the endless days of leftover turkey creations. But things were a little different when I was with The Ex and helping her to raise her two children. Suddenly, my awareness of what Christmas meant changed.

During this time, my staff and I cleaned at the refuge in the Devon area. On one of the days, I was cleaning the communal kitchen areas and noticed a young girl of about eight years old with her mum. We were not supposed to have too much social interaction with the residents, so I was trying to keep a low profile. But the girl noticed me, so I said hello. Conforming to inbuilt rules of politeness and without thinking, I asked them both if they had enjoyed their Christmas. This was a stupid question to ask given the circumstances of where they had spent their Christmas, and I was regretting the question before it had fully fallen from my lips. It was like those moments where you bump into someone in a difficult environment, like at a funeral or in a doctor's waiting room, and we still ask, "How are you?" and respond with the obligatory, "I'm fine, and you?" I can only assume, *I'm fine* is code for everything from *I'm having the best day and I also won the lottery* to *this is the worst day of my life and now I've also realised there's no loo roll and I'm out of tea.*

Anyway, I continued with this agonising conversation, unable to stop the stupid questions from falling out of my mouth. Next, I asked the little girl what Santa had brought her for Christmas. She told me she'd been given a colouring book and some crayons, and she was so happy about it. Her eyes lit up like Christmas lights and her smile stretched excitedly across her face. I, however, felt awful, confronted with the glaring contrast. I had just spent hundreds of pounds on my partner's kids, getting them the latest gadgets, yet they didn't appreciate it like this small girl in front of me with her simple colouring book.

I awkwardly stumbled out of the kitchen area as I had tears rolling down my face. I couldn't understand how this little girl could be so happy with something as small as the gift she had. Every atom of my being wanted to go and buy her some presents, but I knew this wasn't allowed due to their situation. I felt impotent and confused as I headed to my van that evening. I couldn't do anything to help, yet I also couldn't fully comprehend how that small girl had felt so much joy in such circumstances. Stunned like I'd looked at the sun for too long, I drove back to my partner's house; when my sight returned to me it was with the realisation that money doesn't buy you happiness, and it cannot buy you love.

Lesson 6: Children can be the source of truths!

It's strange to know a small girl taught such a big lesson, yet she was blissfully unaware of the change she had created. I will never forget her for the rest of my life. I guess it's true that we can learn so much from children. We can learn to let go of hurts from how kids fall out in the playground one day and make up the next. Perhaps their trust isn't naïve: perhaps we as adults teach them to hold on to anguish. Too many of us are prone to holding grudges forever! Perhaps we should practice finding the inner child and let go, believing that a new day is a fresh start.

Chapter 2: Looks, Personality and Chemistry

Or, why being hot is not enough!

Lesson 1: Looks are the wealth of the young, so don't get too hung up on them!

When we're young, we love looking hot, or at least trying to look hot, and joining in the game of pulling the hottest person in the bar. We put so much emphasis onto looks, yet our looks are the product of our genes and not something we can control. Well, some women attempt to control their looks by taking contouring far too seriously... and apparently men are getting in on this now too! I can't imagine I'll ever walk that path — and by path, I mean the little aisles in Boots where people lunge at you, showcasing their entire product range on their polished faces. It's not that I have a prejudice against men wearing make-up

– it's just that I'm not sure that creating the illusion I have higher cheekbones and a smaller nose will turn my world around.

I mean, looks are the one thing we can't really control and even the best-looking people don't get to keep them forever. Yet my twenty-something self was obsessed with looks. Ultimately, I've now learned that looks aren't the only way to be attractive.

Lesson 2: The obscure flirting behaviour of men and letting men loose in a bar

It's a truth far too commonly practiced that young blokes love being single and going out drinking with the single ambition of pulling a lady. Years later, at my rapidly advancing age, I find the tradition both draining and exhausting, and I might actually now prefer indulging in nap-time. I have discovered there is a very fine line between looking available and looking like you are in the reduced to clear section at Tesco.

It's an ugly truth to admit, but men in bars act like a herd of sharks. We circle around checking out all the women. Then, grouping together, we send one of the lads into the group of ladies. The aim at this stage is to start chatting to the ugly one, but that is a ruse to get conversation going in order to chat to the good-looking lady. It's a strategy we use, but it's the strategy used by ocean-living predators too.

And if you don't have an ugly friend, well, this is awkward... It might be time to take a look in the mirror...

Lesson 3: Men get harassed too!

Now – size is a contentious issue. But before you shout me down for fat-shaming, please note these women have harassed me off the dance floor and away from my beer. That, my friends, is unforgiveable. It's not just men who harass women but it happens vice versa too. Unwanted attention can ruin the night for men too!

My enthusiasm for going out has been somewhat dampened by the fact I seem to be a fat-magnet; not that there's anything wrong with the larger lady, but in the south west the ones who are attracted to me are the same women who are happy to corner the men they're interested in and grope arses like they're checking fruit at the supermarket. I have been left feeling like dinner, or even prey.

But then, perhaps this is how women feel when they're persistently pursued by ageing slime-balls (or sharking lads). I realise men, especially the older ones, don't know how to chat up a lady. They tend to just dry-hump their legs, which is a lot less effective than *hello!*

Sadly, I am also a bit of a freak-magnet too. I mean, you would think the older you get the easier meeting new people should be. Going on dates should be like having a bum-burp: it should just happen naturally; if it doesn't it's shit.

I put my fat-magnetitude down to my aftershave. It was a gift from an ex, and it is called Xerox or something like that, or at least I'm sure it's a copy of something. I failed to notice that it smells like something a farmer might use to wash a cow's udders: *udder-wash* or *teet-dip*, or something agricultural. Anyway, it always attracts the heifers when I go out. It has got to the stage now that when I go out, I take a packet of biscuits with me. When I see a larger lady approach, I scatter the biscuits round as a distraction before making my escape.

It's great though to see the larger lady with bundles of body confidence. In Devon, there seems to be a direct correlation with size and the amount of covering the clothes provide. The larger a Devonian lady is, the less she wears. Or perhaps it's the illusion created when women buy one sized clothing…

Anyway, one lady who bypassed by biscuit trap had a face that looked like it was on the body of a minibus. She made it as clear as a Vegas sign that she was planning on coming home with me that night. I politely declined, but she persisted. By the time I went home I was afraid. I was scared not just for myself, but also for Smirnoff: I don't keep much food in the house, so I was scared he'd end up being a midnight snack!

Lesson 4: Take in the good, the bad and the whole of the person

Anyway, going back to looking in mirrors, I have certainly spent a lot of time mulling over my best features in my reflection. Everybody in life has a good side and a bad side; check your face in the mirror – I can assure you, you will prefer one side to the other.

In the case of Bet Gilroy, she was pretty *up-front* about her best feature.

But I digress. It is true that I am never going to be a male model. But the older you get, looks become less important when you meet someone. Don't get me wrong, physical attraction is still essential, however the emphasis shifts to *clicking*: being drawn to a person, connecting with them. It makes us sound like Lego or jigsaw pieces. But it's true – connection is everything. So, my lesson on looks is don't go for Brad Pitt lookalikes as you might be missing out on someone amazing. It might just turn out that it's not Brad Pitt but Cesspitt who will make you happy!

I've been on dates with ladies who have been quirky in the way they look but I've had the most entertaining evenings. Yet, the evenings I have spent with ladies who are totally self-obsessed have been a yawn-fest! I've often found naturally good-looking people tend to have personalities of a breeze block. Perhaps they've never had to try hard for attention. Perhaps they've never had chance as they've spent more time trying to escape unwanted attention. Perhaps they feel a duty to remain dull to give everyone else a chance!

This lesson seems to work in reverse as well. Women often tell me they don't find men attractive who *know* they are attractive; rather, they prefer men to be oblivious to their charms, or a little humble.

Lesson 5: Being attractive rather than looking attractive

Sometimes, date conversations take a strange turn. One entertaining woman took small talk in a different direction. She asked me the strangest question I have ever been asked and introduced me to the game of *Would You Rather*. She sat across from me, smiling kindly, and asked, "If you were given the choice, would you rather have no arms or no legs?" I almost choked on my prawn cocktail! What sort of question is that to answer? I wondered if it was some kind of psychometric thing where my answer would tell my date what kind of personality I have. Thankfully, I am blessed to have both arms and legs, but the uninvited hypothetical disability felt like a threat – like when a cold caller phones and asks about your recent accident when you haven't had one. Politely, I answered, stating I'd rather have arms than legs. But the questioning didn't end there. Smiling, she then asked sweetly, "Why?" In the sweaty discomfort of the moment, the only answer I could think of was if I were at school and needed the toilet how would I put my hand up!?

I left school 20 years ago!

Mind you, saying that, most kids in my class wore plastic pants anyway. Although, I'm not admitting I did…

Lesson 6: How to cope with bad ~~hair~~ face days

Another thing I have learnt in life is that while there's always people better off than you, there are always people worse off too. This is also true of how good looking you are. I know we're all drawn to looking at pretty people and hating ourselves a little more for being so gruesome. But we must remember to look at everyone else too! I think looking at uglier people can make you feel a whole lot better! So, if you are ever having an ugly day and feeling a bit low, go and visit your local Wetherspoons. One glance round at the spectacle of human misery will have you feeling like an Adonis in seconds! It always seems the regulars in a 'Spoons seem to have given up on life.

A thought: Can looks denote sexuality?

One thing for certain is I could never be gay. Not just because I am not gay – but also because I'm not handsome enough. I know this because I have never been mistaken for being gay. A lady once said to me, "Do you know why it's difficult to find a sensitive, caring and good-looking bloke?" I obviously didn't take it personally that she was speaking directly to me at the time. She continued, "It's because they all have boyfriends already."

I guess she was right: most gay men tend to be good-looking, so I was out of the running early in life. It's safe to say, with my quirky features and lack of style, I will never be mistake for being gay.

Lesson 7: Feeling pretty

It turns out my looks are legendary in my hometown. I remember one time a lady came up to me, with my mates Dave and Shaun. We were at the gym, and she started the conversation saying she knew of us. She said that she and her friends had a nickname for us. She said they call us 'Team Gorgeous'. I was chuffed to bits. But then she went on. She said, "We call Shaun HOT Shaun." And he was like, "Yeah!"

She continued, "We call Dave HOT Dave." And he was like, "YEAH!"

Then, she turned to me and said, "We call you Marbles Matt!"

Stunned, I responded, "Pardon! Don't you mean Hot Matt?"

She said, "No! Marbles Matt." And left it at that.

The reason they call me Marbles Matt is because many years ago I set up a jingles company making commercials for radio with another friend, Rob, and we called the company Marbles. This stood for Matt and Rob's Brilliant Enterprising Scheme. It turns out my company has a better reputation than my face.

Lesson 8: Why lists don't work

I guess looks are subjective. It wouldn't pay for everyone to have the same tastes and likes.

I think as the older we get, both men and women look for different things in potential partners. In my younger years, my desires in women I met online dating were very much looks-based. Embarrassingly, I had a list, and it was pretty specific. In addition to beauty, I was also looking for: 1. Someone who could drive; 2. Was in good shape; 3. Had her own place; and, of course, 4. A mobile phone contract to prove she had good credit history. But lists change over time. Now, it might read: 1. Someone who is female. End of list.

I was talking to a lady recently who was in her late 40s and she said that these days what she looked for in a man had completely changed. On her new list, she didn't mind if a bloke had hair or not. She declared any man was golden as long as he knew not to buy screw-top wines, wore a shirt that covered his stomach, and remembered where the bathroom was. Besides those three rules, she wasn't fussy.

Then, she said the main difference between an ugly man and an attractive man is about 10 glasses of wine. And there was me thinking it was only blokes who had beer goggles.

Lesson 9: It's all in the eyes

Right, after all this ugly-bashing, it's time to talk about my wandering eye. I'm sure in most ways I'm a fairly normal bloke; I have all my own limbs and my bits seem to work. I know nobody is perfect and everyone has a flaw, and I guess my most visible one is my lazy eye. In the past, when ladies have said I have a wandering eye, they are technically telling the truth.

Sometimes, my eye is fine and it lulls me into a

false sense of security. But then, a little bit tired or a little bit drunk and my eye goes off for a wander. Not the cheating kind of wander, but looking a different direction and I can see in front and all the way to my left at the same time. Nothing encourages sobriety like not trusting your own eye! To be honest, I blame the eye test nurse from school. She totally ruined my modelling career! Back in the day, she put a patch on my good eye to make my weak eye stronger. However, she put the patch on the wrong eye... I guess I won't ever join the Chippendales, however I would qualify for the Crippendales. These are a tribute troupe who are made up of people with disabilities. They shake their stuff on stage, taking off their prosthetic limbs as well as their clothes. I could strip off my eye patch... Then I would be HOT Matt. YEAH!

My lazy eye hasn't helped me with eyeing up the ladies at the gym, that's for sure! I was once cracking out my sexiest facial expressions while eyeing up a fit lady who was wearing an all-in-one Lycra suit that fitted perfectly. I strutted my stuff, flexed my muscles and tried to make eye contact with her. I can only assume my eye went to one side and caught the glances of a poor, unsuspecting chap on a rowing machine. Let's just say the poor guy left his workout quickly that day.

That's obviously the only explanation for the hot woman failing to succumb to my charms.

Once, I actually dated a lady who also had a lazy eye. Hers was more pronounced than mine (or at least, I like to think it was). It is surprisingly quite hard work to make eye contact when two people have lazy eyes. In a car at a junction, we were the perfect match, able to look both ways at the same time. But in a romantic clinch we looked like we were having a fit! In day-to-day life we just wouldn't have worked: there was no way I could stop her looking at other men!

Lesson 10: The importance of hair

Hair is another thing that has changed over the years and I haven't kept pace with the trends. These days, people use their hair to make political statements as well as to make themselves look attractive. And I don't mean the hair on our heads, but the hair, or more accurately, the bush down below. Blimey! When I first started dating, some women practically had jungles in their pants and you almost needed to borrow your neighbour's Black & Decker to get through the bush. I felt like Robinson Crusoe at times! I remember thinking one of my former girlfriends was smuggling a baboon in her pants. Then, more recently, everyone trimmed and groomed to the point of adding gems and decorations. I was surprised to learn about Brazilian waxes which leave no hair at all. In one sexual lifetime, we'd gone from one extreme to the other.

And this includes men's hair too. I must admit, since I started watching a TV show called Naked Attraction where contestants pick a new partner by seeing their naked bodies, I am also no longer Chewbacca down below. Gillette shares must have skyrocketed because of the number of razors I go through!

And then, just like fashions, everything went full circle again. Recently, I have read that women are no longer shaving again. This time, the shaving abstinence even includes leg hair. Call me old-fashioned, but I'm not yet sure how I feel about the return to body fur – especially since I have developed my own routine of keeping things smoother. However, with my ageing face and wonky eye, I'm not sure any unshaven women will be too worried about my feelings.

Lesson 11: There's more than one kind of Ugly!

Continuing the talk about hair, I have actually been going to the same hairdresser for about 15 years so she is totally to blame for my look. Locally, she is known as Psycho-Scissors, and she has taught me even hot people can be a disaster. I have sometimes worried she has a crush on me and hides it with constant put-downs when I visit. You know the old adage: treat them mean and keep them keen. Although, with Psycho-Scissors, it's more treat them mean and scare the Bejeezus out of them!

She actually fainted on me once. After helping her to a seat and getting her some water, I asked her if she was alright. She explained she hadn't eaten enough that day and put it down to a lack of sugar. I obviously knew the truth – it was a sign that running her fingers through my hair had made her go wobbly at the knees.

We have our habits and routines. She claims I am the only customer who never tips her and I say the same thing to her every time I visit: "Make me look like a sex object!" She succeeds every time; when I leave her shop, I look like a knob!

Both of my brothers go to her salon too, and she always says to us that our eldest brother is the best out of all of us. She claims he is like the brother she never had, and he feeds the favouritism by saying she is the sister he never had. I think he probably means favourite sociopath he never had and he's just got his words muddled.

I am not being mean either: she is a pretty crazy lady! She has been known to phone clients at their workplaces if they have not been in for a haircut — even when they have never mentioned where they work — chasing them up to make appointments. I have heard of direct selling and marketing, however this is borderline harassment.

Chapter 3: Love is Cruel

Or, how gut-wrenching pain, loss and betrayal

are inevitable. Cheery!

One of the most famous symbols used to depict love is the classical god, Cupid. He is often shown as a handsome and winged deity firing arrows of desire, or as a little cherub doing much the same. I'm going to show you how he is not a symbol of romantic bliss, but of the surety of complete agony. I know I don't need to go back thousands of years to prove that love is cruel; I only need to sign into Facebook and check out some memes and the history of human heartbreak is clear for all to see. A particularly striking example might be, 'Don't fall in love. Fall off a bridge. It hurts less.' But I want to go back in time to show how we've all been fooled.

So, let's get back to Cupid. I often wonder why anyone would think being shot with a love arrow is romantic. Stop and think for a moment: he is shooting people. That is not an act of love; it is an act of bloody violence! In Much Ado About Nothing, a romantic comedy, Shakespeare describes Cupid as 'killing' people with his arrows of love. Killing! You might laugh and sigh, oh! Imagining the cute little cherub with his golden bow, but he's a freaking psycho!

You might think I'm being an ass and argue I've missed the point. You might say they're love arrows – they make people fall in love. In which case then he's drugging people, something I'm surprised the #metoo movement hasn't picked up! Those arrows are spiked! It turns out that long before twats found Rohypnol there were sneaky archers shooting up the dancefloor. I wonder if they were searched at the door before being let in to the *Epulum* (that's a Roman party – I Googled for the name).

Cupid is evidence that for thousands of years we've known love is cruel, like some kind of jape from the heavens, and yet we're still falling for the prank. We're still hooked and will eternally go back for more!

And yet I promise I'm not bitter and twisted.

Lesson 1: We've all been mean

It might sometimes be hard to admit, but we've all caused someone pain. Often, we recognise the pain of being the hurtee, but we have all been the hurter from time to time too.

While this isn't typical behaviour for me, and I'm totally embarrassed to admit this next anecdote, it is 100% true. It was a long time ago, I was about 14 at the time, when I publicly rejected a girl. I guess I could deny responsibility and say I was just a kid – but at 14 you also know the sting of rejection, so I knew what I was doing. I had asked a girl to the cinema. I can't even remember what we went to watch, so it can't have been very interesting. Perhaps I can blame my actions on the poor quality showing. Anyway, about halfway through the film, I decided she bored me and got up and went and sat next to another girl.

I'm still in touch with the first girl so at some point I must have made this up to her. Nevertheless, she never lets me forget it.

Lesson 2: Rejection hurts!

Even though education was largely wasted on me, I did learn a valuable lesson at school on how cruel girls can be. One of my earliest memories of trying to woo a girl was when I was in middle school and about 11 years old. Yes, I really started this love thing young (or, at least tried to) even though I'm still learning lessons now!

At the time I really fancied this girl who was a massive fan of a band called Bros. She told me that if I dressed or looked like the lead singer, Matt Goss, she would be my girlfriend. And as easy as that, the challenge was set! That night, I went home from school feeling anything was possible. I stood in front of the mirror with a picture of her idol, desperately trying to style my hair like his. Oh! The effort I went to. Thank God my mum did not have Facebook at the time, or my humiliation would have been global!

I'd have been a YouTube sensation in no time! But my efforts were not totally in vain – I managed to find an old leather jacket, though I have no idea where it came from. Perhaps my parents have wilder secrets than I know (or care to know either). I went to bed that night all excited, completely convinced I'd restyled myself into a rock star and the next day I would have a girlfriend.

The word 'twat' springs to mind.

I woke up early the next day, giving myself enough time to preen myself adequately. I gelled my hair back like Matt Goss, having perfected the technique the night before. I flung on the leather jacket, and I even put some of my dad's Old Spice on my face – God! It really stung! Think of that Home Alone scene – it's totally true. I think I was blushing all day even before the nightmare to come.

Walking in through the school gates, my new look made a few people turn their heads. But their sniggers didn't bother me as I thought I was a bona fide rock star and I knew the girl would be mine. I'd seen the movies; I knew for a fact how happy this moment would end. However, my moment of romance was delayed as I couldn't find her before the bell. Undeterred, I headed into morning assembly.

I remember walking in and everyone laughing at me. To my shock horror, the girl turned around and saw me but didn't swoon with desire. Instead, with a mocking expression, she said she was only joking.

Oh! I was heartbroken! And humiliated!

But revenge wasn't far around the corner. Since the teen years are cruel, her comeuppance was probably less *karma* and more *kids are dicks*. A couple of years later it became the talk of the playground that she stuck tissue in her bra to make her boobs bigger to disguise the fact she was flat-chested. As we we're a supportive lot, we gave her the nick name Tissue-Tits, and this name stuck with her for the rest of her school life.

I'm pretty sure after Tissue-Gate she started doing the chest exercise which all girls were told if they do it, their boobs would get bigger – it's the exercise where they stretch their arms out to one side and repeat over and over again. *"I must, I must, I must have bigger bust."* It doesn't work by the way!!

Anyway, where was I? Perhaps I got off easy. I guess I can also look at rejection as redirection... flip me! If I had got together with Tissue-Tits, it would have cost me a fortune in Andrex! Mind you, as a rampant randy teen, I used my fair share of Andrex anyway, as I was pretty hands on if you know what I mean...

Then I cottoned on that shooting my load in a sock is just as good and environmentally better.

Lesson 3: Sometimes, there's nothing you can do!

As I'm sure we all do, I have known many people who have had bad experiences with love. One woman I met on a date was dealing with her divorce at the time. She explained her marriage came crashing down around her in a nightmare of lies, and I obviously listened with care. I even tilted my head to one side in sympathy just like my old teacher used to do to me when I ever handed in my work. Anyway, where were we...

My date said she had been married for ten years. She had thought they were happy; they'd had a loving home and two wonderful children. One day, she came home early from work, not expecting anyone to be there. She thought her children were at school and her hubby was at work. But, boy! Was she wrong! Instead, she found her husband in bed... with another MAN! How do you get your head around that?

Being the kind man I am, but not having the foggiest idea what to say, I tried to cheer her up with my sparkling wit. "Well, it could have been worse!" I consoled her over our drink. "It could have been your mum!"

It's safe to say we never spoke again. Obviously, this was because it was all still pretty raw for her and not because I'd put my foot in it.

Lesson 4: Denial can be useful

Rejection can be too bitter and harsh to swallow at times. At these moments, we can always find other ways to explain away the incident to help out our egos.

One of my friends had a date go wrong without even going on the date. She is an attractive and somewhat larger lady around my age. She had arranged to meet a bloke she'd met on the internet in a car park to then go for a drink. Choosing a car park might sound seedy, but that's quite normal behaviour in the countryside where we all need to drive miles to get anywhere. Many of us don't even have a local 'Spoons to go to. Anyway, she waited patiently for her date to arrive. As it was a rural location, there was nobody else there. Then, after a short time, she saw headlights coming closer. A man whom she assumed was her date pulled up in his car, looked across at her through the window, and drove off.

When she told me the story, she explained his hasty exit must mean he had a family emergency. I knew she needed that belief. I didn't want to break her heart and tell her it was probably because he didn't like the look of her.

This reminds me of another story a friend told me where she was the one to instigate a *family emergency*. This friend was on a third date with a guy, and this time they went for a meal. They had arranged to meet at her house, and as she was running a little late, she invited him in when he arrived and left him watching TV for a moment. Over dinner, he had kept going on and on about the size of the TV, insisting it couldn't be more than 28 inches. This annoyed her for two reasons – one, she didn't need mansplaining about the size of the TV she had chosen and bought herself; and two, why did it matter anyway? It was such a boring conversation. Anyway, she texted her sister to need *emergency babysitting* and never saw him again. I wonder if he still believes it was the babysitting that drew her away?

Lesson 5: Therapy is always an option

There are romantic experiences from which there is little chance of total emotional recovery. When confronted with this kind of anguish, the kind of anguish that makes waking up feel like being punched by Mohammed Ali, there are no points for being too proud to ask for help. In these moments, counselling can be an excellent choice.

This was the sage advice I offered a friend with whom I used to work. One quiet day in the studio he told me of a tragic story involving his best friend who lived in North Devon. He recounted that his friend had told him about this time when he was driving home and was dying to go for a poo. He'd tried to make it home, but it was already in the departure lounge so thought he had better find somewhere pretty quick before he accidentally shit his pants. Anyway, he pulled over into a lay-by where they had some facilities. He knew they might be less than salubrious, but he definitely did NOT expect what came next.

He sat down on the toilet and emptied his load. While sitting there, he was shocked to notice a hole in the cubicle wall. Suddenly, a willy poked through! He realised it was a glory hole! He almost shat himself again!

Shouting out, he did up his trousers and chased this person into the car park, feeling violated by the unrequested attention.

But then, he was confronted by a familiar face. The man who'd poked his willy through the wall was his father!

Let's just say family roast dinners have never been the same since!

Bonus lesson: Dick-pics, old people and technology don't mix!

Another story I wanted to share is about the modern-day phenomenon of blokes sending pictures of their anatomy to ladies. I get sexting can help keep things fresh when you are in a relationship, but guys – seriously, do you thinking sending a dick-pic to a lady you have never met is going to lure her to your bed? This is so sadly deluded! Let's be honest, willies are not the best looking of things; do you honestly think a woman will see a picture of your dick and think, *Gotta have some of that*. Believe me, the first thing she will think is, *What a knob*! Saying that, ladies can be just as bad. For example, a friend's mum, a lady in her 60s, was flirting with a man she had met online. He asked her for a saucy picture, so she obliged – however, instead of sending it as a private message, she posted it by mistake on Facebook for the whole world to see!

Chapter 4: Natural chemistry or needing to match?

Or, can a tick-list really find your perfect partner?

I know the age-old adage opposites attract can sometimes work out. Paula Abdul sung about it so it must be true, and she was mad for a cat – it doesn't get more opposite than that! (Although, I would add, it is pretty easy to be mad about a cat. After all, Smirnoff taught me true love!) But typically, I'd wager we need a certain amount of common ground to make it easier to get along. In the long run, if you don't enjoy the same things how are you going to enjoy the time you spend together? Opposites may attract, but I personally wouldn't put my money on a relationship of financial opposites, for example. I know you could offer me many examples of this working, but it only seems to pan out when the richer catapults the poorer to the same financial status, thereby nullifying their oppositeness. The funny thing about opposites is once they are done attracting they often start attacking!

Lesson 1: Different outlooks are future obstacles

I wouldn't say a good relationship depends on both parties always agreeing, but there has to be some synchronicity. Surely, it's harder to create a life together if that life depends on totally different beliefs. From religion to politics or how to raise the children, being able to support each other's world views is essential.

And then, there are important life choices as well.

I once went on a date with a woman from Crediton and I picked her up from her house. When I arrived, she took one look at my cleaning van and refused to get in it. She insisted that she drove. I instantly didn't like her, and I thought: *Who does she think she is?* I've come across a few snobs in my time who have looked down on me for being a cleaner, but it turns out perhaps I just wasn't *hip* enough!

Being polite, I jumped into her car only to find what can be described as a drugs den! It stunk of weed! And whether I was comfortable with this or not, or comfortable with the idea of her driving while stoned, it was too late! I asked her how far we had to drive as I was getting high as a kite just being in there. She wanted to drive to a country pub 10 miles away, however I thought, *Stuff that*! Instead, we went to a local pub in the town so I could make a quick getaway!

Her profile name online was Eco-Warrior and to her credit she described herself as being 'laid back', which I now realise is code for 'stoner'. She asked if I'd ever smoked drugs and when I answered no, she gave me an entire lecture about how it has medicinal benefits. I sat, holding the inside of the door for my life, and decided she was a loose cannon with mental issues. In the flesh, her appearance was more like Swampy – can you remember the guy who protested against a road being built in the 90s? She looked like a tree-hugger! But she was also very pretty. It's a truth you often find most Eco-Warrior activists might dress weirdly and be odd but they do have pretty faces.

Perhaps cannabis had made her a little too chilled out as it turned out she didn't even have a job. This made me think it was ironic that she was so snobby about my van. It was also interesting that she wasn't impressed by my cleaning business – she looked like she could do with a good wash! It made me laugh that she thought she was so laid back because she smoked cannabis but was anxious enough about appearances she refused to get in the van – clearly, drugs don't work!

Lesson 2: Ordering off a menu can be a sign

Another time I took a girl out who happened to be called *Attention Seeking Vegan* but was what I would now describe as an *attention seeking idiot*.

Now, I have nothing against veganism, and I don't

think all vegans are attention seeking. But sometimes these two things intersect, and sometimes it happens in Devon. This one time, I happened to meet her and invite her out for a meal.

We sat across the table and perused the menu. At this point, the importance of the menu hadn't even occurred to me. I went straight for a favourite: but when I ordered my steak and chips, I saw her give me a look of disapproval. Despite the waiter being stood right beside us, she asked if I'd ever tried halloumi, and suggested that would be a more suitable option as she didn't want to witness me eating a cow in front of her. Slightly embarrassed but open to trying something new, I thought okay, I'd give it a try. She then proceeded to preach to me about how vegetarians live nine years longer than meat eaters. Trying to not take it personally, I tasted the halloumi…

Holy sheep's cheese! It tasted like salty shit!

I then told her maybe she should set up a campaign called 'Stop Vegetable Abuse'. I expanded how this was because I once found a carrot and a marrow while cleaning a ladies' public toilet. It appeared both vegetables had met a different end than the one the '5-A-Day' campaign intended. She didn't find that funny. She didn't laugh when I cracked my one and only vegetable joke either:

What did the vegetables say at the garden party?

Lettuce turnip the beet.

I didn't see her again. Not just because of the withering look and the guilt trip in front of the waiter – both very good signs – but also because of how she misrepresented herself. What annoyed me most was that she informed me during the meal that she does actually eat meat. Her justification was that she ate animals with two legs and not four. I was like, is she George Orwell in disguise? She wasn't even a vegetarian let alone vegan!

Attention seeking vegan my arse! I wouldn't date these again! Anyone who tries to control your menu choice is off the table.

Lesson 3: Fashion matters

After one break-up that took a while to get over, I decided to be more open minded about people I met. So, I got chatting to a black girl online. Apart from The Welsh Asian copper, who you will meet shortly, I have never been on a date with a girl of colour. This might seem weird to some of you, but Devon is an almost entirely white county.

I arranged to meet her in Bristol which was where she lived. She was a couple of years younger than me and very attractive. However, I noticed she had a wart on her hand when she sat down with her drink – this didn't put me off as I was a new man! First impressions always last – even the ones we can't help – but I was endeavouring to overlook my normal responses to small things. I had to see through people's disabilities, particularly when they're willing to overlook mine. So I concentrated on her beautiful face instead and tried to enjoy the moment.

But some physical things are hard to ignore. I had turned up wearing tidy blue jeans and a nice shirt. My mum would say I looked *presentable*. Some might say I looked like I'd walked out of an M&S advert; I would take that as a compliment until I remember their food is definitely sexier than their menswear collection. My date, however, turned up in some sort of hip-hop gangsta gear. She was even rocking a baseball cap! There might not have been many years between us, but it was clear culturally we were so different. She was from the hood, a woman with swag and style and INTO HIP HOP! Even though I think I'm up with the kids, or down with the kidz (I'm never sure which one it is) I can't help that think hip hop at my age means hip replacements. Ultimately, I'm a man from a small town in Devon which is affectionately known as Hovis Town – perhaps I gave up too soon, but in my mind, it was never going to work! It was like mashing up Emmerdale with NWA!

Lesson 4: Trust your senses

I know I am about to come across as very judgmental (as if I'd proven myself to be the most progressive thinker so far in this book). Believe me, I am nothing special to look at and always rely on my personality to get me through. Although, that might explain why I am still single…

But the smallest details can put you off. The next woman I met stank! In many ways, she was amazing! She was Egyptian, stunningly attractive, and a doctor. She had been living in England for seven years and her English was better than mine (do you remember what I said about school? I wasn't lying). She was interesting and hilariously funny. But there was something about her that meant I just didn't fancy her – and that something was her smell. I'm not sure if it was the smell of Eau de Chastity Belt, but it was unusual, and it was overpowering. You know how what people eat can make them smell a certain way? Well, I would worry about what she had been eating to make her smell like that!

You learn something from every date you go on, and often what you learn is about dating. However, she talked about experiences I could not have imagined. She had been married previously when she lived in Egypt and it was an arranged marriage. To top it all, she was married to a bloke for 18 months who was impotent and couldn't get it up. How bad is that? Your family fix you up with a dud! Perhaps it was a deliberate attempt to stop her from having any sex at all! What cracks me up is how arranged marriages are such a bizarre concept. All your life you are taught to not talk to strangers and suddenly you are expected to sleep with one!

Try before you buy does have its advantages! After all, you don't expect to buy Rice Crispies and find they've already snapped, crackled and popped!

Although with my track record of trying to find a woman to be my wife, perhaps an arranged marriage would have given me a better chance of success. I do at least have something more to offer than the impotent guy! Mind you, saying that, I'm not sure I would trust my parents' judgement in making a match. They would probably set me up with a 40-year-old church-going virgin. Her bits would be less welcoming than a camel's nostrils in a desert storm. You would need more than a cobweb brush going down on her: you'd probably need to call in Dynorod.

I had another date where my sense of smell was the deciding factor in the relationship going no further. Although, this time it was completely in my imagination.

This was one of the few occasions where the woman asked me out. She approached me in a bar, and after a little chatting, she asked me out for a drink. She was lovely but the only way I could describe her physically is as Postman Pat-Head.

She was very much into dogging... as in owning lots of dogs and spending all her free time taking them to shows and events. I am decidedly a cat person and I'm not sure I could date anyone with a dog. It's not that I don't like them, it's just that dog people often stink of their pets. From that moment, I swear I could detect the faint warmth of damp dog about her.

Plus, call me over-imaginative, but I also had visions of taking her out in my van, and while driving along she would enthusiastically hang her head out the window like a dog. Although, in fairness, I don't think there's a better image of contentment and complete happiness than seeing a dog's face hanging out of a car window when it's driving along (I don't mean the dog driving, of course).

Talking of Postman Pat: did you know even he has a wife and kid now? Back when he first appeared on TV all those years ago, he just had his black and white cat called Jess. She was his only company and would travel around in the back of his van while he stopped off to every old person in the village, dropping off large packages. Now he is married! Did you also know Postman Pat's real name is Patrick Clifton? I often drop this little useless fact into conversation on dates; who doesn't love a Postman Pat fact?

Lesson 5: Always ask about hobbies on the first date

Sometimes it's the not the way someone looks that puts you off; sometimes it can be something they do. I once met a girl in Newton Abbot who was about ten years younger than me. Rather than some hot younger woman situation, it turned out we just didn't click from the outset. I just didn't fancy her. She wore what I would consider to be too much fake tan. I realise fake tan has become part of a normal make-up routine, along with contouring (although, I've only learned what contouring is during the writing of this book). But I would say it gave her the skin tone that Dulux would have named *A Rusty Bag of Spanners*.

However, the biggest turn-off came when we talked about hobbies. Granted, my admission that I work too much to have hobbies, but I love my pet pigs, might have been just as off-putting to her. When she spoke about her hobby, she told me that she was a Majorette.

An adult Majorette.

I didn't think anyone did that after the age of 10. It put me right off!

But, if I'm honest, I think I was also worried my mates would rip the mick out of me – so I didn't tell anyone about this experience. I suppose they're all going to know now though. And having had a chance to process it, I guess she does have experience of handling a large baton! Perhaps I rejected her far too hastily!

Chapter 5: Dating Etiquette

Or, how not to embarrass yourself too quickly

Although the rules for dating have changed over time, some things always remain true. These rules have become apparent to me as I've got older – mostly because meeting someone when you're young is easy. Youth has powers of which it is not aware, and finding love easily is one of those powers. It's probably good we don't know how powerful we are when we're young as we're also really stupid then too.

Lesson 1: Dating habits of the young are BAD!

Okay, I admit it. I engaged in many of the embarrassing rituals of growing up that are frequently mocked in films. Routines such as practicing kissing on a pillow were a norm for me as for many other randy teenagers. But I am also from a generation where if you fancied a girl you had to pluck up the courage to ask her out or get one of your mates to tell her that you liked her. I guess now everything happens through the screen of social media.

It seemed so much easier finding love back then. Well, it was easier to find girls back then anyway. Every nightclub would play slow songs at the end of the night so you could drag a girl to the dance floor. My mates and I called this the erection section: at least you got a dry hump out of it... but dry humping aside, it was another way to meet someone.

Anyway, moving on to further reminisce the shame of my youth: I found it easy to pick up girls. You might consider this impossible after you read the next few paragraphs, but it was true for a time. Those were the days when we didn't have mobile phones or dating apps, so if you wanted to phone your girlfriend you had to walk to the end of the street to use a phone box and hope that a parent didn't pick up the phone on the other end.

My mates and I would use the corniest chat-up lines. Blimey! I have used some horrific ones often inspired by the amount of alcohol I had consumed. They ranged from: 'There's a party in my pants and you're invited' to 'I'm looking for treasure, can I see your chest?'

I am holding my head in shame as I type this.

I even once referred to a girl as a theme park, then dug myself in even deeper when she wanted me to explain. I went on, "You're not like Alton Towers, love, where everyone has had a ride; more like Wookey Hole..."

I guess this leaves corny and dives right into embarrassing.

I also remember once telling a girl that I worked on an oil rig and that she should make use of me as I was only back for one night. Looking back, I think she probably thought, *Thank God!* My friends also recall me telling a girl I was a Peruvian llama jockey and that I was a great ride. I'm not sure how I wasn't arrested for harassment! Another classic was: 'Did you buy that dress in the sales? As it's 100% off at my place.' I used to talk so much crap back then. Some would say I still do.

Lesson 2: We all have dating regrets

The worst thing I did when I was younger, aside from cinema-gate, was see two girls at the same time. However, it taught me to never do it again – there is just too much admin involved! It's true what they say: the truth is always the easiest to remember. Trying to remember what each girl had told me messed with my head. How people are serial cheats I will never know!

The ridiculous thing was I couldn't decide out of the two which one I wanted to be my girlfriend. Yes, I genuinely puzzled over them as if I was choosing new jeans. I did all the usual nasty tricks: I drew up a list of pros and cons of each one, however that was pretty even. I can even remember the list: one had her own house, one didn't drive and so on. Their positives and negatives counter-balanced in a weird way – I suppose that is the nature of people. So, eventually I realised doing a list was probably not the best way of sorting which one I wanted to be with. And if one of them had found the list, she would have been rightfully offended.

So, in some kind of Inbetweeners-like nightmare, I began to imagine the best way to solve the problem. I thought to myself, what if they just had a fight and the winner gets to be with me? Mind you, not only did that sound prehistoric, but it also meant them finding out about each other. This became a running theme through my ideas. I considered setting up an It's A Knock Out-style competition where I'd set them different agility and mental tests.

I suppose the easiest thing I could have opted for was to take them both to the park and give them 60 seconds and see how many twigs they pick up in this time. To be fair they both looked like dogs – it was the 90s and poodle hair was all the rage. Plus, at least then I could see how flexible each of the girls were and what stamina levels they had – for breeding purposes obviously. (I know: romance level – high).

How is this for Karma though: in the end, these girls both found out about each other and dumped me without a second thought. I went from two girls to no girls, and I deserved nothing more.

MATT'S 10 RULES FOR GETTING DATES AND KEEPING THEM:

1. Timing is everything

January is normally such a busy time for dating sites as people make New Year's resolutions and put extra pressure on themselves to meet someone. This can mean finding a lot of new people online at this time. But I also personally think going to the pub in January is the best time to meet single women the traditional way, as in January it's normally only single people or weirdos who go out.

2. Know your flirting techniques

I love to watch people and it's always entertaining watching blokes trying to grab women's attention in pubs. The following are a few of the most common tactics: firstly, there is the stare tactic where they look away at last second when the woman returns the glance. Then there is the age-old bumping into a woman when trying to get a drink at the bar. Or there is the sharking tactic I described earlier. If you are a single woman and you are attractive, you must always take an ugly mate as a wing woman. We blokes rarely chat up good-looking women. Instead, we circle around you like sharks before sending in one of the lads to start the chatting.

3. Use smart strategies to meet people

One smart strategy that I have heard students use during freshers' week is to have a traffic light system for their outfits when they go out to the pubs. For example, if you are single you wear green, if you are in a relationship you wear red and if you are unsure or open to persuasion you wear orange. I think this is a great idea! Wouldn't it be great if everyone adopted this policy? Imagine doing your weekly shop in Asda – you would think you were in singles-heaven with all the staff there wearing green!

Although it would dramatically limit the wardrobe.

4. You don't always have to reply even though it's polite

This rule is probably most relevant to meeting people online, but I imagine the same rule could be applied to texting too, and even when someone random just chats to you at the bar or in a queue somewhere. It is important to remember you do not have to be polite and reply when you get approached by people, especially on dating. I used to have the rule if someone messaged me regardless of age/size/colour/ interests, I would always reply. I thought was good manners. So, when a 24-year-old girl with learning difficulties contacted me, I replied to her message. She had written, 'Hi – I really like your picture', so I gracefully accepted her compliment and replied, 'Thank you. I'm a little bit old for you, but I hope you find what you are looking for.' However, she replied again: 'I really like your picture', and continued to bombard me with messages, which ultimately became quite awkward. I did not want to be rude, but at the same time, it was clearly distressing her that I wasn't continuing the conversation. It turned out, sadly, that I was apparently the only bloke to ever reply to her on this site. But it taught me a lesson – be careful who you speak to. Plus, on a dating site, you should really only be making conversation with people you might want to date.

5. Once you have your date, prep conversation in advance

Conversation should just flow, and in a perfect world it would. But an awkward silence can toll the death of a promising date. So, it is always good to have a few conversation starters in your back pocket. One friend said she always likes to ask questions; the easiest way to get a person talking is ask them questions about themselves. Who doesn't love talking about themselves!!

However, I have been surprised sometimes when meeting people how much women like to be open and personal even on a first date. I typically try and avoid subjects like sex and babies, however, if you are on a date with a lady in her 30s and she hasn't had kids, one of the first things she will ask is if you want them. I suppose it is only natural as it would be pointless starting a relationship with someone if you had totally different outlooks to family life.

One conversation no-no is never ever talk about an ex too much – even better if you can avoid talking about exes at all.

Some dates have told me about their sexual fantasies on a first date before which I found weirdly forward. One lady once even asked me if I liked wearing women's underwear – as apparently her last boyfriend did! I wasn't sure if this was forward or a no-no! And I was too stunned to ask! Call me prudish if you like but knowing how much women's pants have changed over the years, slipping on a thong certainly does not appeal to me! I've even had women ask me if I like wearing fancy dress during sex. I said I once dressed up as Yogi Bear at a kids' party. I'm not sure this is what she meant; I expect she thought I was some kind of fur-vert! I can't see it being a turn on in the bedroom: *"Hey hey hey! Boo-Boo! What do we have here then? A pick-er-nick basket?"*

Like with me practicing kissing on a pillow. One lady bragged to me on a date that she had perfected giving men the perfect blow job, however when she first started out, she literally thought you had to blow into a man's willy – still, you have to start somewhere in life. Technically it should be called a "Suck-Job", so you can't blame her for this error.

It's also strange how certain topics will frequently come up on first dates, almost predictably. Once the polite topics to get to know each other have been explored, such as what you do for work, hobbies, and your family breakdown, it is quite common to be asked what star sign you are – which I find bizarre. I have never really believed any of this stuff, and neither do most of my female friends (unless I just don't pay enough attention in everyday life). But on a date, suddenly the destiny of our stars aligning becomes relevant. I'm a Taurus – and the look on some girls' faces when you reveal this information would suggest I'd just revealed a penchant for peeing on women in the shower. Some put barriers up straight away, and say, "Oh! Our stars signs are not a good match!" In my opinion, the stars and planets do not affect our lives in any way – except the fact that knowing I'm a Taurus has killed any chances of seeing each other again. Talk about a self-fulfilling prophecy. Although, apparently my stubborn refusal to accept it might be important is very Taurean behaviour.

6. Smile a lot

Smiling is a good way to make yourself approachable, to look like you are having a nice time and to help yourself relax. All these things can help sway the awkward and nervous start to a first date and ensure it is successful. I confess I've never had a problem with smiling: grinners are winners has always been one of my life's mottos. But then, perhaps I should have taken that woman's advice to give wearing women's underwear a go... They do say wearing tight underwear makes you smile: it makes your cheeks go up.

7. Make eye contact

As previously mentioned, making eye contact has always been a tricky one for me due to my lazy eye. My wonky eye aside (literally) making eye contact is so important on dates as it shows the person you are interested in what they are saying. The only time this rule has really backfired on me was when I met a lady who was cross-eyed. Her eyes were all over the place, while one of mine was watching the next table. Well, to cut a long story short, after twenty minutes of making eye contact and following her eyes, I was completely hypnotised! I was totally subdued for the rest of the date. Thank God she is a nice person – she could use her powers to rob people blind!

8. Make your own mind up over who is going to pay – there are no definitive rules on this

I guess these days it doesn't matter who pays as long as everyone is respectful in the process. I, myself, am still a bit of a traditionalist and like to pay on the first date. I consider myself a gentleman so therefore I like to treat a woman with respect, and for me, paying is part of that. Not like a bloke I once knew who charged his date petrol money to drop her home.

9. Gratitude can be a thank you, not a shag

There is some debate over what is expected in return for a man paying for a date. I only expect some gratitude in the form of a *thank you*. As my dad always says, 'manners don't cost anything' (I know you're gagging for more of his wisdom).

To demonstrate this, I'll describe how gratitude can make a difference. A while ago, I took a posh lady out. She was very attractive, and she knew it. At the restaurant, she ordered what she wanted and made sure she ordered the most expensive bottle of wine she could. All of which is fine, but it was the tone of expectation that unsettled me. At the end of the meal, she said, 'I'm off to the loo. You can pay for the meal while I'm in there.'

Her manner of entitlement, that I was lucky just to be in her presence, made me think, *Who the hell does she think she is?* I paid for the meal, but she didn't even say thank you. At the end of the date, she said to me, 'I'll message you next time I'm free so you can take me out again.' If I could post a gif here now, it would be one to show eyebrows raising to the ceiling. That night I sent her a text: 'Just to inform you, I'm looking for a girl with manners. As you clearly have none, THANK YOU for showing me what type of girl I shouldn't be dating.' She replied, saying: 'I don't understand, did I say something wrong?'

I thought to myself she must be as thick as shit or so precocious she makes Verruca Salt look humble. She might have the looks, but she had no gratitude. It's a shame I didn't have a night of passion with her as I could have wiped my willy on her curtains on the way out! Although I guess that would look a bit weird. Just imagine it: *hang on a mo while I reach up to your window a second...*

10. Don't put out if you don't want to (or do if you do)

Sex in the 21st century is a lot more liberal than it was in my youth. One-night stands are now acceptable, and the key word is consent – there are no rules if it is legal and consensual. However, I am still a bit more traditional and I have only had one and a half one-night stands. I don't even kiss on a first date, but saying that, things can sometimes get a little wild. Once, I had a woman lick me like a Labrador on a first date.

But my conservative approach to sex hasn't always worked out well. I once dated a personal trainer from Weston-Super-Mare. I was seeing for her about ten weeks and she seemed lovely. She was about eight years older than me, very lady-like and good company.

She certainly played the waiting game. She didn't let me sleep with her until we had been seeing each other for 10 weeks – and I liked this at the time. But then when I slept with her, I worked out why she didn't put out in the early stages! Oh my god, she smelt like a Brixham trawler down below! I nearly got hold of the makers of Febreze to see if they could do a special plug-in air freshener for ladies that whiff! I'd call it Febreze Fanny: I think the alliteration adds a ring to it. Saying that, I am partial to the smell of tuna...

You should also bear in mind this might also get you blocked on some dating sites.

Chapter 6: Dating – The Good, The Bad, and The Bearded

Or, how Nando's isn't the only place to go

for a first date

Dating, whether it's with someone you met online, or on a blind date, or met in a supermarket, or even with someone you already know, can be stressful. There are so many things to think about that the first date has become like an interview. Jerry Seinfeld once famously said something like the only difference between a *date* and a job *interview* is there are not many job *interviews* where there is a chance you'll end up naked at the end *of* it.

If you're at a speed-dating event, it is literally an interview.

Stereotypically, there's plenty of books and

magazine articles for women who worry about what to wear and want to look good. As a man whose version of *nice* is a clean shirt and some aftershave, I'm not sure I'm fit to judge the advice these books and articles give, but since so much of it focuses on looks, I can't imagine it's all that useful. After all, relationships are not built on looks alone (unless you're a 70-year-old billionaire who wants a pretty girlfriend to see you through, but I'm pretty certain the looks criteria is not reciprocated). However, in terms of dating advice for men, there's not much out there. The market is empty – so, girls, perhaps that's part of the reason men seem so bad at it... (eh hem, excuses, excuses).

What follows here are some dating lessons I have picked up that might be of use to you. I have tried to steer clear of how to dress, but one or two outfit-related anecdotes might have slipped through. One thing I will say though, is don't wear a football shirt on a first date. Apparently, you should also avoid wearing the colours yellow and pink; a survey was done, and women state these are the least attractive colours on a man on a first date. For the life of me, I can't work out why – perhaps it isn't true...

Lesson 1: Two's company; three's a crowd

All you need in life is love and everybody is looking for it. It sounds lovely, doesn't it? But what love means can vary from person to person; or indeed, it can vary from person to couple. For example, one lovely date engaged in that often-to-be-avoided topic of conversation for a first date, and talked me through previous dates she had been on recently. Memorably, she recounted the couple of hours she had spent with a bloke she met online; apparently, he had taken things a little further than she was expecting. When they were chatting on the website, they had got on well. He seemed lovely so they agreed to meet. But once at the pub, chatting over a glass of wine, he surprised her in a way she wouldn't want under her tree at Christmas. Boldly, he announced he was already married and wanted her to swing with him and his wife. She nearly choked on her pinot grigio. I guess it's not classed as cheating if his wife watches!

Lesson 2: Always chat on the phone before you meet if it is a stranger

A lady I dated a couple of times told me about an experience that took her by surprise; apparently, the hardest thing about the date was trying not to laugh! She explained the guy she met was pretty hot and she had been looking forward to their date, but then he hadn't really stood a chance after he first opened his mouth. She said he had a weird, squeaky voice, like a chipmunk crossed with a Kardashian sister. Funnily, they didn't see each other again. But they were mysteriously greeted outside the bar by a few dogs.

Lesson 3: Location, location, location

Choosing a place to meet for the first time is a task riddled with challenges. The most obvious advice tends to be to go for a drink for the first meeting to keep it short and arrange to meet again if it is going well. Often, people mention that it should be a public place, and somewhere familiar. Nobody really talks about lay-bys...

Now, I only have this information because it has been reported to me. I swear I have never suggested this myself. But several women – dates and friends – have mentioned that men have asked to meet them in lay-bys. I don't know where this idea came from, but it implies they're only after one thing...

To share a lift!

Joking aside, I'm not sure which is worst – that a lay-by date either suggests a quick shag with a stranger, or an ideal kidnapping and murder opportunity. Either way, a lay-by is NOT a prime date location.

Choosing a location can also be an issue when the woman gets to decide – which normally is the done thing, as if you let the lady choose the location, she will feel more comfortable in her surroundings. Saying that, needing to be comfortable can work both ways. I remember once a mature lady was chatting to me online, and I was a little unsettled because I swear she looked just like Myra Hindley! I mean, this association started as a vague resemblance, but she really freaked me out when we started trying to arrange a place to meet! I think she was trying to reassure me because of the age difference. But actually she made everything worse when she said that she wasn't looking for a relationship, just someone for company to go walking on Exmoor! Yes, that sounds like a great place to go – somewhere isolated and alone and with lots of ditches!

My inner safety voice whispered, *Count me out on that one, love.* Mind you, it would be a great title for a book: *Sex with a Serial Killer!* I'm not sure I'd be brave enough to research that tale though…

Lesson 4: Friends don't always know best

The worst day of the week when you are single tends to be Sundays, but they pale into insignificance against Christmas. To combat this feeling, one year I decided to go on a first date on Christmas Eve. After the initial introduction, I arranged to meet the woman in question and take her out in Sidmouth. This wasn't someone I had met online, but a blind date set up by a friend. A friend I had trusted, but now it's fair to say we have some trust issues.

"Oh, you'd be perfect together!" she had enthused to me! And I had trusted her, not even questioning for a second how well she knew me; I fully believed she wanted the best for me and for her female friend. She said this woman was from London but visiting her family in Sidmouth for Christmas. "What have you got to lose?" She closed her argument with a win.

If I was to put a finger on what went wrong, I'm not too sure what type of woman she thinks I am suited to. I can tell you now, a blonde bombshell who isn't afraid to show off her assets is not someone I am normally drawn to. But apparently, I have miscommunicated that at some point, and on this Christmas Eve, I was paying for it. For a first date, overt sexuality can be quite alarming, and not necessarily for the reasons you might expect. Although, in fairness, the customers in the pub in Sidmouth were probably as much to blame...

I picked her up from her family home, and I can only describe her as a younger version of Dolly Parton – she even wore a leopard print top which only enhanced her milk jugs! The briskness of the December night did not help matters! I've heard of smuggling peanuts but flip me! This was like smuggling walnuts!

Now, I was trying to talk to her and get to know her, but the outrageous flaunting of her body wasn't just aimed at me. Whenever she walked through the pub every bloke stopped and stared at her breasts. Now, you might argue that they shouldn't have been ogling her, which is true. However, I think she was actively seeking the attention as she found a reason to walk dramatically through the pub many times! I read somewhere once an article that started, 'If only women paid as much attention to their boobs as men do...' Well, I don't think the writer of that article had ever met my date as she clearly paid full attention to her boobs.

"I get a lot of attention when I go out!" she observed innocently.

I wasn't sure what to say in reply, so trying to not appear too pervy and weird, I said, "Thank God for that! I thought we had entered a gay pub and they were looking at me!"

I mean, she was deliberately laying her sexiness out for all to see. She certainly wasn't shy in any way, and this was exemplified by her innuendos, which got progressively more awful as the night went on. You, dear reader, might say they were almost as bad as mine, but I refute that! They were certainly as bad as any truck drivers' calls to a women through their van windows.

"What's Santa bringing you this year?" she asked, licking her lips. "If you're lucky, I might pull your cracker!" I wasn't sure if it was a joke or an invite. I was quite scared if I'm honest. I thought, *This is one bird I won't be stuffing this year!*

We spent a couple of hours together, and it was kind of entertaining watching all the men's heads turn as she went to and from the toilet countless times. She maximised the impact on these startled spectators by pushing her chest forward and walked like she had a hedgehog in her pants. Although, I suppose her shoes could have been uncomfortable!

I have the seared impression she loved attention. I guess everyone does to some extent. There's also the chance I got the right impression and all she wanted from me was a Christmas jiggle. But I was looking for love, and if the shoe were on the other foot, I wouldn't want someone to get with me just because I've got an award-winning marrow in my pocket!

Blatant boobage aside, she was also good company. When it came to the end of our date, we even had a cheeky Christmas kiss, which is totally unlike me on a first date. It wasn't inspired by her cleavage, however; I have a theory that girls with wonky konks are the best kissers. She sported an ever so seductively slightly wonky nose, and I was curious to test my theory. In all fairness to her, she could snog! And after all, it was Christmas! But it didn't go any further than this.

Another time, a former boss of mine at a radio station where I worked decided that I would be perfect to date one of her friends. Hesitant after the nightmare of the Christmas Eve blind date, but under the pressure of a friend who cared, I agreed. She set me up on another blind date, and I dutifully went along.

I went to Bristol, and we met in a pub... I'll say more about the pub in a moment! I was worried what she would be like, but no amount of worrying helped me predict who I would meet! After a short wait, a biker woman turned up – all in leather. No word of a lie. She wasn't a catwoman-esque vision in leather either, or even some kind of biker chick. Nope! Honest to God! She looked like a member of ZZ Top. Beard and all.

I thought this had to be some kind of stitch-up. I asked myself, why would my boss think this woman would be my type? To make matters worse, or perhaps it made matters more predictable than I realised, we met in a pub which looked like a Hell's Angels pub! I should have guessed when I saw a spit barrel at the bar.

At the risk of sounding snobby (and God knows I have been judged by snobs many times), but it was pretty rough – I mean the kind of rough where bulky men murder and eat twiglets like me, not the kind of rough a person might mean if they read the *Daily Mail* and wanted to judge a poor person. The bar was complete with sticky carpets and even the barmaid had three teeth and a tattoo of an anchor... on her face!

After this date I vowed to myself I would never let anyone else set me up again.

This was made doubly awkward by the fact my friend was also my boss. How was I going to tell her I wasn't into her friend? Determined to not ruin my career at the time, I told my boss I wasn't fully over my ex. I even exaggerated somewhat, stating it wasn't fair to date anyone as nice as her friend while I was still grieving. Of course, this was all lies, and I will go to Hell for the deceit, however I just couldn't tell her that her mate was as rough as a badger's ass!

Lesson 5: Always check on the single status

I guess typically we imagine that people know when they're dating someone who is already attached. But I have learned this isn't always the case – I once went on a date with a woman who I called Mrs Paranoid-Pants. She was attractive and intelligent, but failed to mention she was already married until I was on the date with her. She was like a pigeon, pleasingly for my writing, as she was all suspicious; she kept scanning her head around the pub, looking to see who was there and if anyone had noticed her.

Wondering what was up as she seemed on edge, I asked her if she was okay. She then revealed she was married. Now, in truth, I didn't stay long after this confession as I was annoyed. But I did stay long enough to ask why she was cheating on her husband.

I don't know what answer I was expecting, but certainly not the one she gave! She said that her husband had cheated on her, and so she was getting revenge. She didn't want to leave him as they had kids, but she wanted to even the playing field.

Stupidly, I didn't ask if that meant cheating in secret or whether she wanted to be found out. Like, was the pub we met in her local haunt? I shudder now to think she might have been waiting for her husband to walk in, and not, as I thought initially, trying to avoid him.

How does the saying go? An eye for an eye will make the world go blind! Well, I think it should be amended to a cheat for a cheat will give the whole world gonorrhoea.

Lesson 6: Curiosity might have killed the cat, but it also killed romance

Talking of paranoid, I once went on a date with a lady in Clevedon, although that wasn't why she was so messed up − at least, I don't think it is. She was the perfect age, in her mid-thirties, and I was really enjoying our date, up to a point. She came across quite normal, however the date sadly went a weird direction.

We went to a local pub for a drink, and it was going well. After a while, I went to the toilet and just happened to leave my phone, drink and wallet on the table, which is also a normal enough thing to do. When I came back, I was, to speak in a very British way, a *little* bit shocked to find this woman going through my phone.

Obviously, my first response was to ask her what she was doing. I expected an apology, maybe some embarrassment. But no! That would be far too predictable. Instead, she went for broke and attempted to plead not guilty. She responded with, "I quite liked the look of your phone and was just seeing what model it was."

You might consider that excuse a believable one, but no person in their right mind and with all the facts – which we both were – would fall for it. As an excuse, it was flawed from the start by the fact that my phone was not even last year's model! It's not an iPhone! It isn't rose gold in colour. True, it does have some smart features, but they are smart by name not by design! I just thought, *I'm sorry but what language are you speaking? It sounds like bullshit to me*. My dad, with his constant wisdom, once said to me, "The most dangerous liars are those who actually think they are telling the truth."

Lesson 7: Lying will set your pants on fire! And not with passion!

The night of phone-gate reminds me of another lady who tried to use lies to gain my attention. Let's start with the fact that nobody is perfect in life. I accept that, and I know that about myself. But this woman clearly could not accept it and was determined to force everyone within her vicinity to bow before her perfection. She was an older lady, so perhaps she was anxious to impress – but the verb she achieved was to terrify!

It was a strange irony that the sign I remembered seeing as we walked into the pub said: *Dogs Welcome*. My date talked so much rubbish and forced it upon me with such aggression, she reminded me of a cross between a bulldog and a shih-tzu!

I don't mean to be disparaging – she was a nice enough lady in some respects – at least until you paid attention to what she was saying. She claimed to be a former model. Let's just say her appearance screamed that the Salvation Army jumble sale had done well that week. Or perhaps she'd been hit by a bus since her modelling career, as I couldn't see the attraction. Although, models these days are often fairly odd looking and super skinny – but she wasn't either of these things either.

Then she said that her Vera (I discovered that was what she had named her vagina) has been featured in many doctors' journals as it is perfectly formed. Now, I don't have a vagina myself, but I'm not sure there is such thing as a perfect formation. But equally – what a strange lie!

Maybe it wasn't so strange as I was slightly intrigued to know what she meant by 'perfectly formed'. But then, she was also somewhat older than I had expected. Judging by the wrinkles on her face, even if her Vera had been perfectly formed once upon a time, I wasn't convinced it would be now! Which reminds me, did you know that up north when a lady goes to the toilet they normally say, *I'm just off to wet the lettuce*. I am ashamed to admit I had visions of a dried-up cabbage with wilted leaves in her patch. That's just not an image of a perfectly formed vagina; it's also not an image of a perfectly formed coleslaw!

So, I'd say perfectly formed Vera, my ass – but also, how cool would life be if liars' pants actually did catch on fire.

It's funny just recently I've been getting a lot of wax build up in my ears, I'm sure this must be nature's way of stopping B.S. entering my head.

Chapter 7: Speed Dating is doing it quickly!

Or, how to meet lots of unsuitable partners in one night and end up alone anyway

Lesson ~~One~~ ~~Two~~ On Its Own: Speed Dating is not for everyone. It might not be for anyone!

Did you know, speed dating is an actual thing? I always thought it was just something that made a good comedy sketch on TV; but I was wrong – it is real. I'm not sure how practical it is for actually meeting someone you like, however it is a very practical way to meet several people in one go.

And to let them all know simultaneously that you

are desperate.

And to quickly learn that they are too.

It's a riotous lark of a way to spend an evening! You should give it a try!

Back in the days before we had online dating, we had primitive ways of meeting new people. These ranged from Ceefax personal ads to newspaper personal ads (also an actual thing). We had supermarkets doing singles shopping nights, and we also had speed dating.

I tried the latter. I didn't find romance, but I did have a laugh.

Speed dating is normally a social event that you can attend with a friend. I don't know if this is because nobody takes it too seriously, so it's nicer to be sociable, or everyone is blooming terrified so you need company to get you through it!

I dragged my friend Pippa with me. To be fair, she had put the idea into my head to try this social experiment, so it seemed only fair that she should suffer it with me. Pippa is lovely; she is very attractive, kind and intelligent, and it's hard to understand why she is single. Well, it's hard to understand why she is single until you get to know her, that is: she does seem to wear negative knickers in life. I'm sure if she changed her underwear and wore positive pants she would never be single (I mean, we now know finding love is super simple really). It's a well-known mantra to say there is a solution to every problem in life, but I think she misheard and now believes she has a problem for every solution.

Anyway, we toddled off to Exeter full of high

hopes and giggles. I was the designated driver so Pippa could have a few drinks – I thought it might help her relax a bit more. We were ready to meet our dates for the evening!

We arrived at a bar and before the event started we got to mingle with the 20-odd singletons (as in 20 or more, rather than there were 20 people who were odd). As I stood at the bar, a bloke walked in on his own and ordered two double vodkas. Making conversation, I asked, "First time here by the looks of things?" assuming the vodka was for his nerves.

He replied, "No, it's my seventeenth time."

Ruddy hell! I thought. *That's not great advertising for the event!* I wondered perhaps the truth was even worse! Perhaps he was a terrible date! Surely after that many times, you would realise maybe speed dating isn't for you!

Anyway, the concept is simple: the ladies stay seated on individual tables and the blokes have three minutes with each lady. You then make notes before moving onto the next table in a pre-organised direction and meet the next lady. At the end of the night if both the lady and the man have ticked to say they liked each other, contact details are exchanged.

Clear and easy – *What could possibly go wrong?*

Now, three minutes might seem like a very short amount of time, but Einstein showed us that time is relative. And it relatively sped up and slowed down erratically throughout the night. Three minutes didn't seem long enough with some women, however, with others it felt like a lifetime. The first girl I sat with was a classic example: I didn't know how to approach her to begin with, so I took the lead and asked her lots of open-ended questions about herself. However, she was so shy that you'd find more life in a dead badger! She didn't even ask me one question in return!

I was so thankful when the three minute bell rang; I scurried away. Sitting down at the next table, I said, "Sorry, I have just got to quickly make notes about contestant number one." Trying to not be too distracted from the outset and spend too long writing, I simply wrote the words *Nut Job* as a reminder that we hadn't clicked. It turns out you really must be careful what you write. The new lady in front of me, who I hadn't yet even introduced myself to, read the paper and took immediate offence. Unbeknownst to me, contestant number one was her best mate!

It didn't get off to a good start! But I still hoped I wouldn't need 16 more goes to get it right!

However, after the first two ladies, things did not improve. Lady number three certainly didn't get the concept that you are supposed to have a conversation with each other to see if you like each other. Instead, she took a more interrogative approach. She reeled off quickfire questions, making assertive eye contact and not hesitating on the answer before firing the next. It was like being shot with an exam!

What's your favourite colour? What's your favourite film? What kind of work do you do? What hobbies do you have? What kind of music do you like? And so the questions continued. I didn't answer half of them, and she was going so quickly, I'm not sure that she noticed.

But then came the *pièce de résistance*. She asked, *If you could be animal which one would you be and why?* Well, when you are put on the spot you don't really have time to think about your answer, sometimes you find yourself saying the strangest things. I replied, "Elephant," and I should have stopped there. But I didn't. Instead I tried to think through the answer and allowed my mouth to keep talking. I cannot explain why the next thing I said was the first thing that came to me, but it was. The very first thing that my brain deemed acceptable to say out loud was, "So I could give myself blow jobs with my trunk."

It would appear this was not the answer she was looking for. And perhaps in hindsight it was not the answer I wished I'd given. My new favourite answer to this question for if ever I am asked it again is to be a *goat as* then I can say I can walk around all day with a horn!

I did meet some lovely ladies that night in all different shapes and sizes and with different intelligent levels too. I met a really posh lady who was stunning, but I was never going to click with her as I am as rough as rats! (I've checked – that is the official terminology.) She was a redhead and she was so posh she named her hair colour *Coppery Spectrum.* I said it looked ginger to me which didn't go down too well, but since the time was running down quickly, we moved on. I noticed she spoke with a plum in her mouth and had enormous teeth which were shiny and white. They stood out, like she'd put a comedy distortion Snapchat filter on her mouth and then the wind had changed direction…

She was nice to speak to though. We spoke about where we'd each like to go on holiday. She wanted to visit Gambia and places far away to get to learn about other cultures. I thought, *Flip me! I'm not taking you to Africa, love; they'd poach you for your ivory!*

Finally, as the event was reaching its climax, I reached table number 10 where my friend Pippa was sitting. She was completely intoxicated by this point, suggesting my plan to keep her relaxed was a little misguided. I asked her how her night had been, and she said every bloke had bought her a drink. She then hiccupped that she had forgotten to make notes, so now couldn't remember much about them.

My sheet had detailed notes come the end – well, detailed for me. They included *Nut Job* for table 1, *Elephant girl*, *Posh-ginger-teeth-bird* and a number of other equally useful descriptions. At least I knew who was who, and I did actually tick the boxes of two ladies I wanted to see again.

Drunk and confused, Pippa ended up ticking everyone's boxes.

The journey home was memorable for all the wrong reasons. One minute, Pippa was talking drunk boy talk which is annoying enough. You know the chatter: "What is wrong with me? Why can't I get a boyfriend?" she cried out! The next minute she was fast asleep. Then, suddenly, she started making weird noises, and we all know what that means was coming next! I stopped the van quickly, not really thinking about safety anymore, happier to crash than to be covered in drunken puke. I pushed her out of my van and she vomited on the roadside. What a way to end the night!

How is this for Karma though? A few weeks later, she arranged to meet one of the guys she had met at speed dating, even though she couldn't remember him. She had no idea what he looked like, who he was, or anything about him. It was total drunken payback as it turned out this man had a nervous twitch. Apparently, it was quite off-putting. Think Trump with Tourette's.

Neither of us met our true loves that night. But I did meet up with one lady I met. At the event, I found her engaging, attractive, and well-dressed. She was chatty and friendly – mind you, we only spoke for three minutes, so I suppose I didn't have much to go on really. On our date night, she was nothing like I remembered. She didn't wear a lot of clothes and had loads of tattoos. Not that I have an issue with body art, however it was like being on a date with a Hell's Angels drag act. As for her work, she was a prison officer! She also had very hairy arms. We didn't see each other again.

Chapter 8: Sexy Time

Or, on dirty sex, weird sex and always getting

consent

It will probably not come as a surprise to you to see that the chapter about sex is the largest chapter in the entire book. One way or another, we are all obsessed with sex. From the earliest stages of our sexual identity when we are consumed with *getting it*, to over-analysing whether we are getting enough in our long-term relationships, sex is a big part of our lives. It impacts how we present ourselves, our clothing, our life choices and whether we show our sexuality and wealth off in some materialistic version of peacocking. It gives us power while simultaneously being the source of power-removal all over the world. Over the generations, with the advent of contraception and modern medicines, as well as evolving sexual liberation, we have gone from judging a person for being promiscuous to now being able to label a million and one sexual identities. Since now bisexuality and pansexuality can co-exist with separate meanings, it seems we are subdividing our desires in ever-increasing detail like some kind of infinite spirograph drawing. Heteronormativity, aside from being a challengingly long word, is becoming the new missionary position; old-school, boring and predictable. Is there any way to define a healthy sexual relationship anymore? Well, please let me try…

A metaphorical evolution of sexual relationships that go from '*sexy first date*' to '*can't take that back even if you wanted to*'

A friend of mine explained to me how she went from having a hot and promising date to receiving TMI (too much information – but you knew that already) in a few short weeks. I believe this story is a lesson to us all about perfect matches and the importance of chemistry – and how those things are not worth *shit* if you haven't got a sound relationship to build them on.

My friend recounted her tale of woe, which all unfolded after meeting someone on Tinder. At first, he appeared to be a normal bloke. He was attractive and they had fun together; making the next date had been easy and she had eagerly awaited each one. But then, chinks began to appear. After a few weeks her date started subtly dropping things he liked sexually into conversation. He started with things like, "Sometimes during sex I like to have a carrot inserted up my ass."

I think this is the point alarm bells would have rung for me and I would have legged it as fast as

Forrest Gump on amphetamines, however, vegetable abuse aside, everybody is turned on by different things. So she persevered. She jokingly quipped, "Well it's one way to get your five a day!" And I realised, joking aside, to her vegetables in bottoms was well within her bedroom boundaries.

Then, a week later the subtlety began to slide like a mudbank on the edge of a flooding river: he informed her he wanted to have sex with a lady-boy. Again, not being judgemental, she just thought, *Each to their own,* and carried on seeing him. She was pleased he felt comfortable enough to share his desires with her.

Ultimately, she needed a hefty jolt of smack-in-the-face indecency to push her over the edge. The thing that finally made her realise things were not quite right was something that happened when they went for a naughty weekend away in Bristol. Everything started out well, and they enjoyed a wild night of passion. But, unbeknownst to her, something had gone wrong. The next morning, she woke up and he was gone. Before she had chance to consider where or why, she noticed he had left her a parting present. For some reason, he had gone and done a shit on the bedside table!

I'm sure you have plenty of questions right now. I do too. Sadly, I do not have the answers. This is largely because she did not contact him again. I can't even tell you if she cleaned up the shit herself or left it for the cleaning staff... I'll know the answer if she refuses to visit that hotel again.

But the one thing I do know, no matter how promising the date, no matter how much things seem to work, if you're not into the same sexual pleasures, it's all going to be shit in the end!

PART 1: MY EARLY AND IMMATURE (MIS)UNDERSTANDING OF SEX

When I was young, I laboured under some serious sexual misunderstandings. Thankfully, I have learned and double-thankfully, for many of these issues I learned quickly. This section might be better for 17-year-olds beginning their sexual journeys, but I hope you can enjoy them too.

Lesson 1: Sticking it in isn't enough

I am embarrassed to admit that I used to think I could satisfy a woman by merely sticking my love dragon in her cave. Well, that was very wrong. Women like a bit of teasing and foreplay – and there are many skills to develop in these areas. I mean, blimey! Every single woman is different, and it is important to find out what she likes and how she likes it. Back when I first started out, I used to think just adding a bit of spit to a Vera was all that was needed to gain entry – these days, I know you have to work for the main meal. Anyway, where were we? Okay... yes: This is why sex in relationships is often so much better than brief flings and one-night stands, despite the fact this is contrary to the movie-promoted idea that the first lust-filled bump and grind is an orgasmic explosion. Often, this is totally not true.

Lesson 2: Be honest about your sexual history

A strange but common behaviour is that new partners lie about how many lovers he or she has had previously. I have heard about men who have exaggerated their sexual history to sound like a stud. I know one bloke who used to claim he had slept with over 300 women, which seems impossible in a small town like where we live. Funnily enough, when he got with his girlfriend who is now his wife, he changed his history to double figures as he didn't want to put her off.

But women can be just as bad as men; one woman I used to know dated a friend of mine and told him she was *practically a virgin.* As a description, I wonder what that really means – was she trying to appear chaste? Or saying she was prime for mythical sacrifice to a dragon? How can you be *practically* a virgin – either you are or you aren't. Can you imagine the pitch for a bride in an arranged marriage...? *"She's almost perfect! She's only slept with one person, and he came quickly, so she's as good as new..."* I wonder whether she was saying all her experiences were so bad in her mind they didn't count. Perhaps she had good reason – in reality, she'd be able to compete with the 300 guy for real! I'm sure she was actually just worried he'd be judgemental and think she was a *Loose-Moose,* or as my gran would say, *Margarine-Legs – easy to spread.*

Lesson 3: Age is sexy

The best sex comes with age. A couple of times in my

life I have enjoyed flings with older ladies. When I was 21, I met one memorable lady who was at least twice my age, which I guess is every young man's fantasy. She gave me the best blowy I have ever had. Although, I am not sure if this was to do with the fact she removed her dentures beforehand (although, that seems less funny now I am that age).

Lesson 4: Masturbation DOES NOT make you go blind

There is an age-old rumour that having a pull can make you go blind – I wonder who thought of that? Did some poor sod have the misfortune of going blind one day while enjoying his morning glory? Or did some sicko parent think the best way to scare their son was to threaten blindness? Or perhaps some idiot teen came in his own eye and freaked out... I don't know how the Old Wives always get the blame for these fears, or even who the Old Wives were, but either way they were wrong. The truth is, tugging has health benefits. It has been scientifically proven the more orgasms you have as a man the greater the reduction of risk of prostate cancer. Apparently, it's all to do with the harmful toxins you flush out when you ejaculate – so men, get to the shower! You don't want those bad boys to build up!

PART 2: THE ORIGINS OF MY SUCCESS

Romantic locations:

Before we get too deep and meaningful, as sexual conversations tend to be, let me take you back to the very beginning. I think it's important to note that amazing moments are not always perfect. Losing my virginity was awesome, terrifying and perhaps a bit of a non-event... As I am going to explain a little later, I've only had 1 ½ one-night stands, and in a clumsy sort of symmetry, my first time was also only a half. It might have even been a third!

Despite the mathematics, the occasion was certainly memorable. It all happened in a little yellow metro. I was very young, and she was quite a big girl (certainly for the space available inside said metro). The reason for my fractions is that I am not even sure I was inside her; I could have been humping her belly button for all I knew! That would certainly explain the fluff on my willy the next day.

But seriously, our brief liaison is something I have thought about a lot. When I die, I don't want to lie in my coffin and look back with regrets. Although I'm not sure what I will be doing in my coffin – probably having a tug since there's not much else to do, and at least I will be stiff already. I'm sure I will have some regrets, like I already regret not having a baby thus far, but if I am honest the biggest regret in my life to this point is my first sexual experience. I mean, I didn't even know the lady's name. She dropped me home after I met her in a night club; I met her way after the *Erection Section* as the night came to an end.

Terrible to admit, I didn't even fancy her; I gave in to peer pressure from my mates as they had already tested their rockets. I thought to keep in with the crowd I should also blast off!

The sex was nothing to shout home about, though you might have guessed that since I couldn't distinguish between her vagina and a belly button. I've heard that metros were built for comfort and not speed, but I'd seriously question that now... However, if I look at the positives, I did get a free lift home, which was a bit of a result. And just in case I was inclined to forget, I also got a scar on my shin to remind me of the occasion.

I'm sure you're now gagging to know more. As you can tell, I have never written a book before, but I will endeavour to recreate the scene for you. I was at the number one night spot in Devon at the time: Verbeer Manor. It was the happening place back in the day; it remained the number-one night spot until The Cook Report did a drugs raid and it was shut down. Good times!

Anyway, even back then I attracted the chubbier lady. The metro lady took a shine to me when I was stood outside the club at the end of the night eating a kebab – I'm sure you can picture me now looking like a fast-food-eating, drunken god. I'd like to think it was me she was interested in and not just because of the food I had to offer. Some girls like free drinks, but free food is a lesser known pulling technique.

One of my mates pulled her good-looking friend, fulfilling the stereotype that good-looking girls always have ugly friends. We stood around uncomfortably for a bit waiting for our respective mates to stop snogging. I kept eating my kebab and made small talk. Then she said, "How about I give you a lift home?" I'd heard a rumour about the rule that lifts lead to sex, but I also thought about how it was a cold night so I thought if the rumour was wrong at least a lift might be nice. But my suspicions were correct; she had her eye on more than just my kebab.

She pulled up at the end of the road near where my parents lived. Even if she'd been super skinny, there wouldn't have been a lot of room in the metro. She leant across and kissed me; it wasn't the best kiss in the world – it was complicated by the pointy end of the gear stick and the fact I was still wearing my seat belt – but she seemed to know what she was doing, so I closed my eyes and went with the flow. I remember that she started stroking my face, and before I knew it, she had her hands down my pants.

I was like a dog on heat, dry humping like a nutter. I wanted to look like I knew what I was doing, however I didn't have a ruddy clue. She climbed over to my passenger seat; well, I say climb, more like rolled. It wasn't exactly like the beautiful people at the lookout points in Hollywood movies. The truth was, despite the cold, I had to get out the car at this point so we could get into position – talk about sex gods (and I think it's safe to say you wouldn't be talking about us).

With a little adjustment, I got back in the car. After sliding off my jeans, she pulled up her dress. It was enormous and further complicated the available space. If I'd been into asphyxiation, or even known what that was, I'd have been having a whale of a time. I felt something wet and warm against my leg and then she directed me inside her, or inside her belly button – depending on which version of the event was true. Blimey! They say some women are hard to get into, like carrier bags used to be in supermarkets where you had to spit on them to get them to open up; well, this was more like a bag for life – I went in with ease! That probably highlights my lack of skill – and totally shows why I can't work out which hole I was in.

To this day, I still don't know if I lost my virginity that night or my dignity. What I do know is the next day I didn't feel like a man; I felt dirty and confused. However, in the eyes of my mates, I was no longer a virgin – I was a MAN!

The Half-Night Stand:

As I've mentioned, I don't like one-night stands and have only had 1 ½. The time has come for me to tell you about the half. Many years ago, I went on holiday with my friend Rob. Aren't holidays where all the best sex stories happen? There or in yellow metros anyway. We went to Cyprus, and spent the majority of the week behaving like The Inbetweeners, getting drunk and trying to flirt.

One night, in the hotel bar, we got chatting to a Welsh Asian copper (which is a bit of a mouthful, and it meant she had a beautiful but unintelligible accent). Rob looked like he had pulled her, and I was gutted because she was extremely pretty. I spent this part of the evening like a third wheel and was looking around for distraction. When it came, it came at the expense of loyalty. Let me confess. When Rob excused himself to go to the toilet, I mentioned to this woman that Rob had bladder issues; I spoke seriously, telling her that he weed into a bag and that he needed to go and empty it. When Rob returned from the toilet, I'd won her over; she was finally more interested in me than him.

Did I feel terrible about this lie? Yes… Did I take it back? Did I heck! All is fair in love and war, and besides, Rob had already forced me to sunbathe on a remote beach next to a dead goat… sadly, that is a long story and it's not on topic – so to find out more you'll have to wait for my next book!

Cut to a little later in the evening in the cheesy discotheque. I was dry-humping this poor, unsuspecting Welsh Asian copper when she whispered in my ear, "Wanna come back to my hotel room?" Like a bunny rabbit in spring, I hopped to her call.

I was about to encounter my first proper one-night stand; she looked stunning. Vaguely, I remembered something a friend once told me: *if you ever go down on an Asian woman, take water with you as they are a bit spicy*, but I dismissed the thought, thinking neither of us had been eating hot food. So, there we were, exchanging tongues, when she took control. She pulled my clothes off and pushed me to the floor; she was quite forceful, but I was too drunk to notice the alarm bells ringing. She didn't take off her clothes at first. Instead, she put a flowery dressing gown over her clothes before proceeding to take her clothes off from underneath. This was new to me in my inexperience, but I put it down to shyness or a cultural attitude to nakedness (not that I was thinking in coherent words while lying there drunk and naked).

She then hopped on my love dragon and started riding me like Tigger with full on enthusiasm. Up to this point, things were going well: I was definitely in the right hole, she was gorgeous, and we weren't freezing in a car with levers sticking into places that no knob should be. She seemed to be making all the right noises, albeit in a hybrid Welsh-Asian accent which was a little hard to follow.

But then, she surprised me one step further: she started dirty-talking. Now, I hadn't ever experienced pillow talk before, so I had nothing to compare it with, but as far as I'm aware it's not typical to start talking about your dead husband while riding a bloke you met in the bar. I tried to blank out what she was saying and stay with it, but it killed the passion as quick as if she'd started talking about my parents!

I told her I desperately needed the toilet, grabbed my clothes and legged it as fast as my little legs could carry me.

To make matters even worse, when I got back to my hotel room, I found Rob sitting outside against the door – I'd had the room key in my pocket all along. I confessed what had happened, and that I had only half finished the job. I dread to think what she must have thought; thankfully, we didn't bump into each other again. Rob thanked me for telling her that he used a wee-bag; he said, *"What goes around comes around!"*

It's strange to think needing the toilet saved us both that evening.

PART 3: THE REALITY OF SEX, SUCH AS KEEPING TOILET ROLL BY THE BED

Sex is a messy business. Not only do we have to synchronise our desires and develop the necessary skills to do so, but so much of sex is icky. From the noises to the fluids, and the unpredictable nature of our bodies, sex is not like in the movies. Here, I set out some wisdom I have picked up along the way.

Vaginas sometimes smell. Sometimes vaginas smell nice, and sometimes smells can be changed with something as simple as a shower. But lots of things impact on their smell, from diet to age and health. I have had some personal experiences of this I'd like to forget, but since I can't forget I will share them with you. The first that comes to mind was when I was thrilled to date a woman twice my age in my early 20s; this was one of my fantasies come true. She was amazing at blow jobs, as I pointed out earlier, but I also learned that some fantasies should stay just that! When I tried to repay her generous and fabulous skills, she smelt of death! For posterity, I'm going to name her after a flower; let's call her Forget-Me-Not because I will never forget that smell.

No matter how women groom, hair grows back; and some women keep a full bush. There was another girl I saw for a while who just oozed sex appeal. I worked with her and dated her for a short time. Everyone fancied her, and I suppose I thought I would be the first in the office to get her – God, I sound like a jerk! After a short while of dating I went back to her place. Oh! When I went down on her it was like eating my way through a jungle! Ruddy hell! Chewbacca from Star Wars came to mind. She was just so hairy! I have never been into sci-fi ever since.

Size does matter. The best put-down I has ever had was from a woman who told me I was the fourth biggest willy she'd ever had. Initially, I took this as a compliment as I wrongly assumed she had seen a few. But apparently, I was the fourth biggest out of the five men she had slept with. I was second to last!

Vaginas are stronger than childbirth. When I was younger, I stupidly used to be put off from dating women who had already had kids as I was worried their bits down below might look like a car crash. How wrong I was! Vaginas are a blooming miracle! Considering what comes out of those Veras, they pop back like they were designed for it! Perhaps this is where bloke humour creates a bad reputation: I have a mate who said that you should never watch your partner give birth as it's like watching your favourite pub go up in smoke.

Orgasm shapes and faces are weird. I remember one time that I was getting jiggy with a woman on the bathroom floor. We were full of passion and the sex was intense. Now, don't get me wrong, I know my own orgasm face is probably no picture. I can't even imagine what happens to my lazy eye. But there we were in my bathroom and the woman responded like she was having an epileptic fit! I wasn't sure whether to be proud or to call an ambulance! I'd never seen a girl react like this before and didn't know whether staying *on board* was the right thing to do! After, I wondered whether she'd been lying on the toilet duck! If orgasms can happen like that, I don't know whether to have sex more or never again!

Foreplay such as fingering is a technical skill. Despite the clumsy obsession with fingering as a teen, I had no idea how much skill there was to learn. Blimey! It's an art form! And it is well worth noting it can only be learnt with experience. I didn't have a blinking clue when I first started out. It's not something your parents teach you either. I have wondered how much easier life could have been if my mum had brought a fresh chicken back from the supermarket and gave me a lesson in this important subject. Although Sunday dinner would be weird after. I can imagine my dad now: "*Darling, why is the chicken smoking a cigarette?*" On this topic, there is a famous joke and it is funny and dreadful for good reason: *What do a clitoris, an anniversary and a toilet have in common? Blokes always miss them.*

Periods are messy. I remember waking up with a girlfriend one morning after a night of passion. We'd fallen asleep naked in each other's arms. The next morning, unravelling herself from our snuggle, she got out of bed to go to the toilet. I rolled back, thankful for the moment of coolness, but I was taken by surprise. I noticed that on her side of the bed were what I thought at that moment to be skid marks. It looked as though she had shit on the sheets. However, it turned out her period had just started.

On a related story, I remember once going to a house party with my friend Nick, cut a long story short, we stayed the night as he had pulled this girl who I can only describe as "The Joker". She had a big smile and wore bright red lipstick. Next morning I walk into the bedroom to wake him up as I needed to drive home for work. I can only describe walking in on a crime scene. "The Joker" must have come on during the night, and My friend Nick must have been giving her the "T.O.L" during the night (tongue of love) his face was covered and I don't mean he had sanitary pads stuck to his eye lids!!!

I once read somewhere about one lady who just lets the blood flow naturally out of her, and I've always wondered if this is a logistical nightmare... I guess she must avoid wearing white trousers. Although, I am aware periods always turn up when ladies are wearing their best panties, and I'm pretty sure women have faked the time of the month to avoid sex with partners.

The importance of good pants. I've mentioned a few times now about how the bush has changed over the years. Well, the size of pants certainly have too! When I was a kid, as far as I know anyway, women wore gurt granny pants, or *apple catchers* as we used to call them. I wonder if that term was just a West Country thing? Nowadays, some women just have a piece of cheese-wire! The pant fabric is so small, I wonder whether they offer any garment purpose whatsoever. They look like they are nothing more than a framing device for the buttocks! I never realized how many different types of pants ladies have – period pants, everyday pants, sucky in pants and they have my favourite "Gonna get some action pants". Now one girl I dated for a short time wore the sexiest underwear ever, it was all lacy. One downside was for some reason her pet chihuahua had chewed most of the gussets. Instead of throwing them away, she kept wearing them. It was terribly off putting when going down on her and seeing chew marks on her panties.

Beer Goggles are not the only problem. I know for women appearance is important – it is a joy as well as a curse in many ways. But for men, women's appearance can result in enormous confusion. Make up and nice hair used to be the only factors that might create deception… and man! Some ladies wear tons of make-up; it's a face – not a colouring book. These days, there are *chicken fillets*, which are small liquid-based pads which are inserted into bras to make boobs look bigger, and Spanx which are pants that hold in body fat and shape women's bodies into hourglasses. It's like we've taken an entirely different woman home!

One of my friends had a surprise like this when he took a lady home one night after he pulled her in a night club. When he woke up the next day, she looked nothing like she did the night before! I'm sure booze had a little to do with it, but there was more than just clothes on the floor; it was like she was some kind of alien and had slipped out of her human form when he wasn't looking! There was a Spanx suit that looked more like a special effects outfit for a movie; a padded bra that had melon-sized pads in the cups (she could rob a supermarket and get away with a week's groceries in those buckets); and even a mop of fake hair! He thought there was a dead cat on the floor at first! But oh! It's just your other person outfit! That's alright then!

If you are not in the zone, don't fake it – just don't do it. All blokes will suffer erectile disfunction at some point on their sexual journey, whether it's through too much alcohol, stress or even lack of sleep. The best thing I have learnt over the years is if you are not in the zone then give up. It's too distressing to try to force the issue. The more you worry about not being erect, the worse it becomes. Sometimes, you just might not be in the right zone. Plus, it's worse for a woman if you try and drag this bit out as she will think it's something to do with her, even when it isn't. So, there is no point trying to force it to happen when the love dragon clearly is not in the mood. Don't see this as a sign that you need to start buying Viagra – this happens to every bloke along the way so panic not! One of my friends told me once, one of the worse things to happen to him when he was giving a girl the T.O.L (tongue of love) – she let out a fart while he was down there… sometimes there are no words!!!

PART 4: PEOPLE ARE TURNED ON BY THE CRAZIEST THINGS!

I have been fortunate to have lived out most of my fantasies over the years. Some fantasies are pretty common, such as the desire for a threesome. But some are a little harder to explain. In modern times, people seem pretty open and happily share their deepest and darkest desires, but many of these desires still take me by surprise. Here, I set out some of the sexiest to craziest of lustful longings.

I might as well start off with a crazy tale… But this is a true story. *The Sun* newspaper went with the headline: Cow Perv Guilty. That says it all really but let me explain. This story is about a man called John Curno, aged 80, who is also a churchgoing man – if ever there were two reasons to not suspect indecent behaviour, you'd think age and religion would be good ones! But apparently, we'd be wrong! John Curno was been found guilty of molesting cows! His punishment is that he has been banned from every farm in this country! Apparently, the farmer's wife caught him not once but TWICE. She explained she caught him with his trousers around his ankles, his left hand interfering with the cow and his right hand masturbating! Now if that isn't a story to make your milk curdle, I don't know what is!

Did you know that some people pay large sums of money for used underwear on the internet? Yes, used underwear! Not second-hand because I'm trying to save money, but still dirty… and for sniffing. I realise I have missed a trick with this as it could have been a real money-making opportunity. However, after thinking about it, even if I could persuade all my female mates to donate their undies, I'm not sure I'd want to be in charge of storing them all and then handling and posting them. How would you catalogue them? Drawer 1: custardy knickers; drawer 2: period pants; drawer 3: skids… (Oh! The mind boggles like mixing popping candy with vomit.)

On a lighter note though, I nicknamed one of my previous girlfriends *Pritt-Stick Pants*! This came about because of an incident that occurred during one romantic weekend away. We were play fighting, and I was winning. Obviously, play fighting is a competitive business. Desperate to regain the upper hand, she threw her dirty underwear at my head. Noticing her change of tactic, I ducked! She missed. And the ruddy things stuck to the wall of the hotel room!

Dressing up and role-playing can be fun! I once joked with a girlfriend that we should have wig sex... but that resulted in some confusion. I don't mean I suggested having sex with wigs. And before you class me as a complete weirdo (although in our modern, open-minded world, I would hope you wouldn't anyway), we already had a box of fancy-dress stuff I have accumulated over the years. In the box I happened to have a ginger wig and an old lady's wig (okay, I'm now sounding weird even to me). I suggested to my girlfriend that I could pretend to be Ed Sheeran and she could pretend to be the Queen (perhaps there's no denying it – I am a bit weird). I think perhaps I misunderstood what role-playing means. Besides, it's improbable that the Queen would want to shag a ginger...

Some people are very open about their pleasures. One of the most shocking moments in my life was when I was carpet cleaning one day. The owner was home; he was a man in his 50s and he seemed pleasant enough. Chatting away, he said on Wednesdays, when he had the house to himself, he liked to dress up as a lady. Obviously, as you've probably guessed, that very day was a Wednesday.

Before I'd even had chance to set up the carpet-cleaning machine, the chap disappeared and reappeared wearing a dress. He burst back into the room and exclaimed, "My lady name is Ruby-May!" I nearly shat myself! Feeling a bit uncomfortable, I went out to the van to pretend to get some more cleaning materials and called one of my workers to join me on the job.

Public loos are a sexier spot for some loving than you'd probably guess. Though, I'm not sure it's a sign of everlasting love. Can you imagine your elderly neighbours nipping out for a bit of naughty on a Sunday? *"Jean! I'm feeling mighty horny today! Let's get down the loos in the park? You know the one, with the suspicious indoor puddle and the faint smell of pee...? No?"*

Believe you me, as a cleaner I have seen it all over the years. Just the amount of ladies' underwear I find in men's toilets is unreal! Someone must be getting some serious action! I feel sorry for the poor women going home without any pants on; I just hope they don't get frostbite on their flaps. And why go in the men's? There are way more cubicles in the women's!

It's not just men who seem to get off on doing stuff in public toilets – in my job, some of the strangest stuff I have found have been items left in ladies' toilets. Once, I found a bag of carrots and one had definitely been sexually abused. Another time I found a marrow! Now that must have hurt! By far the most bizarre thing I found was a dead goat. I don't know if it was John Curno branching out, some kind of sexual sacrifice, or a woman desperate to get some horn! What I do know is that it scared the life out of me!

One distinct joy of cleaning toilets is reading the graffiti. Some of it is intentionally funny, but the number of messages left on doors and walls looking for sex is crazy. Some memorable lines are: *I want to watch while you f@ck my wife,* and *Married Discreet Man looking for rent boy, call this number.* How charming! Another was, *I want to bash your back doors in.* But some of the funniest graffiti was a conversation I witnessed unfold over a few days between two gay guys. Each day a new line appeared. These went:

Guy 1: Looking for 12-inch cock for discreet adult fun.

Guy 2: I'm the man for you, when can we meet?

Guy 1: When are you free? How will I know it is you?

Guy 2: Wednesday 10.30am, I will cough three times.

Guy 1: I want to be your slave, see you Wednesday.

I thought to myself as I read the daily messages like episodes of a soap: *Good golly! If someone goes to the toilet on Wednesday and they have a bit of a cold, they are buggered... literally!* I still wonder why Guy 2 didn't say he would be recognisable by the sausage in his pocket.

Shoe fetishes are a thing! I recently found out a female friend, who is an air hostess, quite often sells her used footwear on the internet! I also found out that blokes tend to buy them for more than the original cost! She says she lists them on eBay with a picture of her legs while wearing them, and apparently that is the key to her success! Apparently, lots of blokes get off on this! I'm not sure I'd get the same price for my work boots though!

Acrotomophilia is a thing. Don't panic; I didn't know what this word meant either. I found out it's when an individual expresses a sexual interest in an amputee because of the missing limb! Now, I once when on a date with a girl with a wooden arm who I had met online (I met the girl online, not the arm – which, incidentally, was hers). However, before you judge me – I'm not into acrotomophilia – I liked the girl when we met online and it just so happened she had a missing arm. I didn't even know about the wooden arm before I met her in person. I was chatting with her and making eye contact and having a nice time, trying to work out if we had any chemistry. After 20 minutes, she said to me, "You're such a gentleman."

Surprised, I replied, "Am I?" She said that I hadn't mentioned her arm. At that point I looked down and no word of a lie, it looked like she had bought her fake limb off eBay. Anyway, I never saw her again. This was not because I'm a Missing-Limbist, but I didn't fancy her. Plus I was still mentally scared from when a lady violated me by putting her finger up my bottom – more about *that* incident later – I had visions of going to A & E with a wooden arm sticking out of my bum.

Chubby chasers: Now I know I already come across as a bit of a fattist, but big can be beautiful and some men are attracted to a larger lady, just as some women are attracted to the larger man, Sadly, as I have the skills of the best at fat-magnetism, I'm just not attracted to larger women. But being big doesn't mean you won't get any action. The horse girl who rents my stables and land is a pretty big girl but she is happy. The first time I met her, we spoke briefly on the phone when she made enquiries about renting my land. She sounded lovely on the phone. It's strange – I've heard some men say, *nice voice on the phone add 10 stone...* (I'm sure that will spoil your image the next time you phone a sex line.) When I met her in person, the first thing she said to me was she doesn't ride much. I wasn't sure if she meant her horse or men. Mind you, there's always that chubby-chaser dating site for her!

PART 5: WHEN THE GOING GETS ROUGH...

As with anything, it's important to know your limits. We all have them in one way or another, and it's crucial to be able to define that quickly at the start of a sexual relationship. This is a lesson I learned the hard way after managing the traumas of a finger up my bum, a symbolic threesome with the ghost of a dead husband and a hot woman in a dressing gown. Anyway, here's some of the things I have learned.

Lesson 1: Anal sex is not for everyone

Anal sex is not for everyone. Despite my lack of interest, I've still had a few anal incidents over the years – and they have been mentally scarring! The first and only consensual experience was self-inflicted. No, I don't mean I stuck something up my own arse... I just agreed to someone else doing it. It wasn't even sexual; I had colonic irrigation. To cut a long story down to size, my girlfriend at the time was on a health kick and was scared of having the procedure done on her own. So, like the wonderful partner I am, I went along for moral support. If I'm honest, I got way more than I bargained for as moral support quickly evolved into having it done myself.

Apparently, Margaret (the nurse undertaking the procedure) was lovely; I'd be concerned that anyone who has made a career out of sticking a vacuum up someone's arse and clearing out their colon cannot be described adequately by the word *lovely*. Primroses in a meadow in sunshine are lovely; despite her friendly manner, she was most definitely something other than *lovely*. She was in her 60s, but she had amazing skin and swore by colonic irrigation as a procedure. She said she personally had three of them a year and put her health and skin down to this routine. Enthralled, I thought if colonic irrigation can help me look that young at her age, what have I got to lose? The answer to that question is my self-respect.

Happy I'd been convinced to have a go, she started prepping to get started. She handed me a gown and left the room. On inspection it was no ordinary gown; it was like a hospital nightie, but it had an anal entry point. I changed and sat on the couch. She had already instructed me to lie face down on the couch and call her when in position. At this point I felt quite comfortable, relaxing to the gentle music playing in the background, which you seem to get at all these health spa places. It sounded like whale mating calls over a gentle melodic piano – that is apparently the official sound of calmness. Or, as I pondered after, the whale song was a useful way to disguise my wails.

"Margaret! I'm ready for you!" I called happily to her; I was so relaxed I could have fallen asleep. But then she re-entered the room wearing latex gloves.

"I'm just gonna check for blockages…" She explained ominously. With that, she shoved a finger up my bum. The feeling of relaxation instantly changed. Good golly! My facial expression must have been something frightening to behold. You know those ancient paintings of Hell with people writhing and suffering in excrement? I think they might have been based on an experience of colonic irrigation.

The next thing she said I will remember until my dying day: "My! You're not used to a finger up your bum, are you?" As if this was a normal daily activity. I can imagine her morning conversation now:

"What have you got planned today, Margaret?"

"Oh, just the same old, same old. Gotta get some milk and some carrots. Walk the dog. Vacuum the hall, stairs and landing, oh! And my large colon." The tone of her voice implied I was some kind of weirdo for not being into that sort of stuff! Was Margaret lovely? My arse!

I replied instinctively in a high-pitched voice I barely recognised, "No! I ruddy am not!" Truthfully, I feared I would never be the same again!

The only other time I felt totally violated by anal activity was several years later when I had a brief liaison with a woman who I can only describe as Parachute Pants. I gave her this name because every time we'd met her pants seemed to be down by her ankles. To say she was hungry when it came to sex was an understatement. In such a short space of time she taught me so much, and it wasn't all good.

The night in question I recall with such clarity; she was staying over, yet the majority of the evening was fairly unremarkable. We were getting intimate and I felt her hand slide down onto my bum. I squeezed my buttocks together to indicate my anus was a no-go area, but I guess my buns are just too firm, so she didn't get the hint. I felt a finger linger, and the next moment she ram-raided me by shoving it sharply up my bum. The gentle lingering from before faded aggressively into hard penetration. She seemed to take delight in watching me in pain; rather than noticing my violent jerk as agony, she asked whether I was enjoying it. I was enjoying it as much as the average person wants a hot poker parked in a nostril! I'm not sure what came out of my mouth; rather than something useful, it must have been something like one of the Bee Gees hitting a high note.

Lesson 2: Some people like a bit of slap and tickle

For some reason, this woman loved rough sex, and it was just something I have never been into. I have never hit a woman before in my life, let alone during sex. But she spoke about how much she loved it and encouraged me to give it a go. Eventually I agreed and said I'd do it.

Even after consenting, I couldn't quite get my head around it. I thought, *How hard do you hit someone?* I wondered whether there was a scale with sexy at one end and domestic abuse at the other. If so, why hadn't anyone told me about it? Surely there should be a Dulux card with the range of bruising on it – *ahhh pale pink; that's called 'Fruity Blush' and definitely part of our Sexy range. Oh, no sweetie. Deep Purple Splatter is just for police enquiries…*

So, the night came. After gently slapping her a couple of times she insisted I hit her harder. The whole thing was so stressful. I was tempted to give her a right hook to the kidneys just to wind her and get it over with.

The relationship didn't last long after that, and the truth is we were not compatible. Also, I gave her the nickname of Kit Kat which didn't go down well. It seemed perfect for her because she liked four fingers and not two. This was another thing I never felt comfortable doing as it felt like holding a naked Sooty doll. Occasionally, I wanted to speak like a ventriloquist, but thankfully I managed to hold that in.

I later found out she was quite known in the town for the whole finger up the bum thing, as if it was her unique selling point. Silly me for thinking I was exclusive; in fact, I wasn't exclusive at all.

She worked for a letting agent, and was well known in and around town. While at the gym one day, I got chatting to a friend, who mentioned he'd heard I'd been seeing her, and said he had a funny story. It turned out he'd been to view a rental property some time ago which she managed, and the viewing had gone in an unexpected direction. Like a terrible 70s porn plot, they'd had sex during the viewing. Also, she had done the same thing to him and stuck her finger well and truly up his anus. This all had happened before I'd started seeing her, and my friend was well-known in town as sticking it here there and everywhere, so I thought I should really get to a clinic to make sure I hadn't caught anything.

Lesson 3: Sexual health clinics are amazing – know where yours is!

This brings me to probably the most embarrassing moment in my life, which was in a waiting room at a sexual health clinic. God! I felt like I was in the audience of Jeremy Kyle; inexperienced and naïve about how much of a service these places provide, I surveyed the room trying to play guess the STD with the people waiting. It didn't occur to me they could be doing the same in return. And I was there because of a finger up the bum after an illicit shag in someone else's house!

After what felt like an interrogation from the clinic staff and a nurse doing an examination, she asked me some more questions. She asked if I cleaned my penis. Surprised, as I thought washing your penis was a common thing to do, I joked and said I used Harpic Toilet Duck as it gets right under the rim… Apparently, she didn't think that was as funny as I did.

Anyway, the swab tests came back with a clean bill of health, thankfully. In retrospect, the questioning was pretty explicit. "Have you had anal sex with a man recently?" they enquired.

I said, "No, but I've had a finger though." Apparently, that didn't count.

A friend of mine regularly frequents a sexual health clinic; so much so, she is on first-name terms with most of the nurses there. I must admit, I find that a bit disturbing, but I guess she is taking her sexual health seriously. According to her own admission, she has had most of the STDs going; the last one was a wart on her left flap… Anyway, where was I?

In summary

I'm a fairly normal bloke (I think anyway — although I'm aware I like to repeat that a lot), but I realise when joking about other people's quirks that we all have them. I admit, like a lot of men, I prefer not to cover up and wear protection when having sex, but in this day and age, you are asking for trouble if you don't.

The choice to not wear protection is another reason that sex in long-term relationships is way better than in one-night stands. There's no better sex than when you know your partner's body and turn-ons so well, the love making is like a beautiful symphony rather than a head-banging one-hit wonder.

It might be a little odd in 2019 to not like one-night stands (granted, my experience of them is both limited and not exactly too spectacular; remember the Welsh Asian copper who loved to dirty talk about her dead husband?) But I have learned you can't always have it your way. I now realise I shouldn't just focus on finding a breeding partner (I mean a woman to share my life with and not a heifer like John Curno would enjoy); I know that sometimes we just need Mrs Right Now.

To sum up, I have worked out what I like and what I don't like. I've never been into one-night stands and I've also never done anything too wild like join the Mile-High Club. Saying that, even if I did it would probably be a solo flight given my luck with women to date. But it's good to know your own mind, and what floats one boat might sink another. I'm sometimes prepared to try new things, but two things are non-negotiable: I don't do buffets or bums. It's an odd mix, I know, but I don't mean together. Although, I'm sure that there's people who love to combine them. I've seen in films that drizzling food during sex can be hot, like melted chocolate or flavoured jellies. But I also wonder if there's people out there playing with Nando's during sex – eating coleslaw off each other's bodies and tearing chicken while rutting away. Oh! That's a disturbing image; I nearly vommed in my own mouth. For me, I can't bear people touching food with their hands, coughing and spluttering over the vol au vents. That's not for me, and neither are bums. I shall leave anal sex to others. For me, bums are for poo and that's that.

When all is said and done, I know love is not a crime; I guess you can't help what or who you fall in love with. So, to close this chapter, I'll conclude that you can't be wise and be in love at the same time.

Moving on…

Chapter 9: Break-Ups, Exes and Staying Friends

Or, on life after love in a small world

All too often, after love has ended, we feel like our world has ended too. From dealing with the bitterness of parting ways, to managing feelings of rejection, confusion or regret, moving on can be tough. It's a time-tested cliché that time is a healer and it's true. However, it's so hard moving from losing someone who was your best friend to the adjustment of them becoming someone you used to know. Of course, if a girl walks away and you love her, chase her as that's exactly what she needs. Although – only to a point, otherwise you quickly become a stalker. From a female perspective, if you're the one stupid enough to be walking away, the lady is normally smart enough to let you go.

After a break-up, often we then have to contemplate a new life: how we fill our evenings, becoming comfortable attending functions alone, booking a table for one when we want to eat out... Plus, loneliness is unbearable for all of us at different times of our lives, and this can certainly be true after a break-up. However, it is better to be lonely than being in a relationship with the wrong person.

Even having the whole bed to ourselves can be a stark truth sometimes.

However, with very few exceptions, we all have had to cope with break-ups from time to time. Sometimes, we are the heartbreaker and sometimes we are the heartbroken. Either way is tough. But eventually we make it through to the other side.

And then comes the anxiety of starting over. We have the double responsibility of having to build a life as a single person while simultaneously looking for love. It is a hard balance to strike to continue to be open to love while also living your best single life. Some people swear off relationships; others succumb to the misery of feeling unlovable. Questions such as *'what's wrong with me?'* fall off the lips of many a wonderful person at our lowest moments.

It is so easy to lose the faith when you are single. It is normal to go through stages of wallowing in self-pity and questioning why you can't find someone normal to love you. And there is a very fine line when you are single between looking available and looking like you're an abandoned pet. While it is normal, it is also miserable. So, let's take a look at the darker side of love so we can truly know none of us are alone. The sad thing is, when you are in your twenties being single is a choice, when you get to your seventies it's a fact of life.

Lesson 1: Dealing with rejection

At some point you will experience rejection in life. We all do. It might not be in a relationship, but to live life without rejection means never taking a chance on anything. I have some useful tips on how to manage that gut-wrenching feeling.

After breaking up, it is easy to mither over all your past relationships, making comparisons. But this is a bad thing to do – put the memory box away and stop thinking about how it must all be your fault. The blame might be yours; who am I to judge? But sometimes you must forget what you feel about the past, and focus on more what you deserve in the future. Plus, I'm not sure how beneficial your groundhog-day analysis of your inability to pick up socks off the bedroom floor is going to be if the only purpose is to make you feel worse. Although, I know we all do it (the groundhog-day analysis, not the leaving of socks on the floor – what kind of animal are you?)

In general, I'm quite an upbeat and positive person, however even I have found myself wistfully reflecting on serious relationships I have been in been in and wondering why I'd not found The One yet. Sometimes you feel like a kid a school and the captains are taking turns picking who they want on their team. More often than not, the ones left to last are the ones that are either mentally, physically or socially challenged. Being single makes you feel like you are in that PE lesson being left to last to be picked. But your time will come again even though it feels like rubbing crushed salt and vinegar crisps into an ulcer (although, I have a friend who likes that pain – she's a bit weird, it has to be said). You must remember, they are an ex for a reason. Although you might not have wanted it to be over, it is important to recognise a relationship will only work when both parties want it to.

So, the first step is acceptance – getting to the point where you can accept it is over and that you are now single again. I think of this as changing rejection into redirection. It's a chance to build the life you're yearning for, rather than agonise over a life that wasn't what you'd hoped. For example, rather than giving into the feeling that something must have been wrong with me, I try to look at how this is a chance for me to move away from something that had gone wrong – even if I'd not been the one to feel it that way. You know the 'we're not compatible' line: it's actually very helpful when used appropriately.

Additionally, it is great wisdom to know that if you constantly look back in life you never really move forward. You can't get where you're travelling by facing backwards. At best you'll stand still, at worst, well, that's a crash waiting to happen. There's a reason rear-view mirrors are so small while the windscreen is so big. Face front and know where you are going.

Whenever things go wrong, the *recovery-decider* is not in how you feel about it, it's in how you deal with it. For example, after a breakup, a lot of blokes turn to alcohol. I suppose women do too, but I haven't mate-checked it as a fact. I guess it's a fairly obvious thing to do: you're single so you're going to want to go out, occupy yourself and meet people – and so much of socialising revolves around booze. But it's a truth of which to be wary: in no time at all, you will be convinced that your ex-lover is dying for you to phone them at 3am. You will know for certain you're at your most attractive, appealing and reasonable while staggering home on your own from the pub.

The humiliation will only add an agonising nuance to the hangover the next day.

Lesson 2: We all have the playlist of the broken-hearted

I don't know if this is the same for women, but whenever I'm going through a break-up, I always listen to the lyrics of songs and they always seem to relate. Yet when I'm happy, I just listen to the music and don't even think about the lyrics.

I mean, you can always tell when a bloke has met a new lady or fallen in love. Not only does his mood change but also his taste in music. Take my brother for example: whenever he goes through a divorce he plays a lot of hardcore rap, heavy drum 'n' bass, and other aggressive music. The moment he meets a new lady, he starts playing Spandau Ballet in his lorry! We can literally tell the state of his love-life from the sounds emanating from his vehicle before he's even arrived.

Although, that sounds like he gets divorced regularly. In truth, he's had a fair share of break-ups, but he's no Ross Geller. Not that he'd care if he was on a break or not.

Lesson 3: Revenge is not always sweet

I have always tried to maintain friendships with my exes after splitting up. Some people seem to do this easily, and yet I know other people who regard their ex as dead to them once the break-up has happened. But I live in a small town, and I think it's better to be civil if you can. However, it doesn't always work out as planned.

I once continued to employ an ex of mine as my bookkeeper long after we split. One week, the only sensible time for her to come round to do my books was on a Saturday. My new partner was at the house, so I decided we would go out so we wouldn't feel awkward. I thought this was the best way to give my ex the respect and space to do my books; and please bear in mind, she had moved on long before I ever did with a new partner.

My new partner and I went for a lovely walk and made the most of a delightful Saturday morning. After a couple of hours, we headed back. Books complete, we said cheerio to my ex and thought nothing more of it.

Unbeknownst to us, while we were out, one of my cats had very kindly brought a mouse into the house. It was a dead mouse. However, it wasn't just dead, it was brown dead. It was *Walking Dead*-dead – without the zombieism. My ex, full of the resentment of meeting my new partner and being left alone in my house, decided to play a prank with the little, rotting corpse.

To cut a long story to the murder-point, later on that night while we were getting ready to go out, my new partner screamed like a bobcat stuck in a trap. She had found the mouse in her shoe, and the cold, damp body had freaked her out. However, she immediately thought it was sweet that one of the cats had taken to her and brought her a present. Although I thought it was odd that my cat would put the mouse in her shoe, at this stage, I knew no different either. And we both laughed about it throughout the evening.

The next day, my ex phoned to check on the work she had completed. Before ending the call, she asked, did my new partner like the mouse in her shoe?

I must admit that I laughed. However, I also thought it was a little mental. I guess everyone is weird sometimes, especially after a break-up. But there is still something to be thankful for: at least she didn't shit on a hotel bedside cabinet!

I really shouldn't have been surprised by the whole mouse-gate incident as a few weeks prior to this, the same ex tried climbing through the cat-flap as I was getting intimate with my new partner. "I know you're in there!" she shouted through the flap. Eventually I had to put some clothes on and answer the door; to say it was a passion killer is an understatement!

Lesson 4: Sometimes chasing is plain harassing

Many years ago, it used to be considered respectable for women to play hard to get and it was expected that a man would chase. While this is often presented as romantic, in recent years, this trope of idealised romance has been pulled to pieces somewhat. Men all over the world have been re-informed: no means no. This isn't just a sexual statement; it also refers to persistent chasing too. But it isn't just men who behave this way.

I once went on a date with a woman who had a couple of kids. She was about eight years younger than me at the time at 32. One of the first things I learned about her was that she had been engaged 7 times; who gets engaged 7 times by that age? That's an engagement every other year since she was 16! The only reasonable explanation that came to my mind was that she was Snow White and every one of the dwarves had hopped on!

But her engagement history wasn't the only concerning thing. In a creepy voice, which might have been an attempt at a sexy voice, she announced she has a problem saying the word NO! She then said that all blokes who go on a date with her want a second date. Always.

Unnerved by the suggestion she was some kind of siren, I firmly decided I didn't want to see her again; however, it took her a while to get the hint. Over the next 24 hours, I had numerous texts from her despite making it very clear I wasn't interested.

Oddly, she even said, 'I'm not gonna chase you for a second date,' but then repeatedly texted.

Finally, I texted a blunt message: 'I am not interested. Goodbye.'

And then she replied, 'Sorry. Who is this?' I've heard of rejection deflection texts, but I could see our conversation above; did she really just want me to think she'd deleted me first? Well… I wish she'd done it sooner!

Lesson 5: Face to face is best

While it's not always possible to have a graceful break-up, you should always make the effort to do it face to face. After all, there are so many risks to breaking up by text. Here's a couple of examples:

Risk 1: You're not on the same page

W – I need to tell you something

M – What is it babe?

W – I broke your Xbox

M – What!!!!!!!

W – And I'm cheating on you and am going to leave you

M – So my Xbox is Ok???

Risk 2: Autocorrect

M – FYI: I'm dumping you when I get home tonight

W – Fine with me. Was thinking the same.

M – WTAF!!?? That was autocorrect. I meant I'm JUMPING you…

W – Awks…

Lesson 6: Ghosting

Ghosting is the art of breaking up by just disappearing and stopping all forms of communication until the person you were seeing gets the hint. It is not a modern phenomenon, but in a world where we are constantly connected, disappearing has become more difficult. Not that I would recommend ghosting as a break-up method; it seems a bit cowardly to me. And it also seems like hassle – I've heard that the ghoster often has to start whole new social media accounts, change phone numbers and sometimes even move towns. Although that just goes to show the lengths to which some people will go to avoid a difficult conversation.

And it's not even just a rumour; I have a friend who came home from work one day to find out his fiancée had left. She had taken everything except the cat (although, it seems heartless that she'd abandon her pet too). Then, I overheard another friend plotting to leave her husband for her new chap; it turns out she was buying furniture for her new house on her husband's credit card!

But the best ghosting story I ever heard turned out to be a much-needed break-up despite the accidental ghosting. One woman thought she had met her perfect match. They talked about marriage, travelled great distances to see each other when at uni, and were planning to get a home together when he disappeared without trace. Six months later, the woman found out he had gone to prison.

Lucky escape. Though not for him.

SECTION THREE:

TAKING IT DIGITAL

Chapter 10: Online Dating

Or, how the internet promises to find your fairy

tale come true

It's funny how life changes. Back in The Day, dating agencies were dreadfully stigmatised. Jokes abounded suggesting anything from desperation to prostitution to finding your own personal serial killer. Next to small ads for men and women with a GSOH sat ads for escorts and massage parlours. I guess if there were no partners of interest to you, you could at least find a way to occupy yourself for the rest of the day...

But then the internet was born, and everything

changed. I wonder whether modern technology is linked to our changing social habits, and whether now we have this tech it is impossible to live without it. We do seem to be less sociable nowadays; our lives are becoming busier and people never seem to enjoy the moment. This is evident in how people act at concerts. They don't dance or listen to the music anymore; instead they get their phones out and record it. Mobile phones have made it possible to Facetime and connect with people on the other side of the world, however we then ignore the person sat next to us. Has this same change made a difference to dating? When we go about our day, are we're so absorbed in our business that we forget to meet people? Or do we just like a computer to tell us we make a good match? Like when we played the name game when we were at school, and the sum of the letters in our names showed that we were an 87% match with our crush.

These days, there are countless dating agencies available for every type of dater. You can find everything from the romantic sounding eharmony.com to the logically named match.com, which could also a be a site for fire safety. There are even sites that explicitly promote your priorities; for example, for a woman looking for a rich man there is sugardaddie.com or wealthy-men.com, and for the hobbyist there's naturistpassion.com. There are free sites with dodgy reputations such as Plenty of Fish and expensive sites with reportedly scientific profiling such as Elite Singles. There really is something for everyone; there are niche sites for people with food allergies and even for people with zombie fetishes. If all you want is a shag, several more mainstream sites have a hook-up section for you, but you might prefer to go directly to the site called I Would Bang You. Why beat around the bush? Unless that's your thing of course...

It also doesn't seem to matter what dating site you join these days as they all seem to interlink. Judging by some of the dates I've been on, my profile has unknowingly appeared on dwarf dating, disability dating, hot to trot dot com for people into horses. I must have also turned up on dog dating, as one woman licked me like a Labrador at the end of the night. I didn't ever try uniform dating, for people who like nurses or policemen, etc. Knowing my luck, I would have met someone who worked at McDonalds.

Anyway, over the next few chapters, I am going to lay my experiences bare and selflessly regurgitate a warts-and-all experience for you – literally.

Am I being cynical about the online dating business? Perhaps. But the truth is an algorithmic match is too simplistic when compared to human experience. Finding love is as hard as ever and it has never conformed to a clearly written out set of rules. However, when you watch the adverts for these sites, they make it seem that people are falling in love every second merely because they share a love of open fires. Life-affirming articles represent the experience as infallibly cute. For example, one love-struck couple in Cosmo magazine joked that they had *matched* by accident as the woman had not changed the age or location options from the default – and by Jove! She fell in love with a man 13 years her senior who lived 50 miles away! What a jolly tale for us all to learn from! And further proof that technical mathematics might not be the answer since they *matched* after incorrectly setting up the profile in the first place.

The truth is modern love stats are no more optimistic for the algorithmic generation than any love-matching method that has gone before. The ONS states one in three couples meet online these days and correspondingly one in three marriages end in divorce – so you do the maths! If nothing else, the statistics show that broadening our love-pool options and changing our meeting strategies hasn't made the results any better. Whether you marry the hot girl in a baseball cap from two cities away or the hairdressing psycho from a couple of streets away, you're just as likely to end up battling over who bought the pans and who gets custody of the pets. (For your information, I will always maintain custody of my cats – and the pigs too.)

Besides, growing up in the pre-internet generation, I never really thought I'd end up looking for love in this way. I mean, it didn't even exist when I was younger. It's hard to imagine a day before Google, but years after my first Amazon Prime account and my first online shopping experience, I still never expected to shop for love online. I see young'uns swiping on Tinder as naturally as me ordering a takeaway to be delivered on a Saturday, but I always thought I'd be married with children by now. I never thought I'd end up strategising to optimise my dating options. Even in recent times, I never thought I would have to resort to such measures.

But after having tried and failed at speed dating, I decided the time had come: I would embrace the digital dating scene.

After this decision, I met a different girl every

week for about two years and became quite an expert at this dating malarkey (or quite a failure, depending on how you look at it). The trouble is you end up talking about the same stuff with each lady, and I'm not sure if that perfects the routine or makes it stale. But, this two-year modern-dating internship has taught me a lot about online dating dos and don'ts. Now, I am going to summarise some of them for you.

Lesson 1: All sites are the same really

Choosing the right site doesn't seem to matter; websites don't have qualities, they have people on them. Just like a town you might visit, meeting people can be fairly random. When I first set out, I thought choosing the site was key to meeting the right lady. So, I decided to go for a paid site. My thinking behind this was simple; I thought it would attract a higher calibre of lady. How wrong I was!

At the time, I didn't want to do free sites as I believed the advertising that *nice* women would be on the *better* quality sites – as if the site itself was like a washing machine and quality can be bought. I also didn't want to use sites that in my opinion had a bad rep, such as plenty of trout dot com, as I was under the impression that it was just a sex site. The reality is that a website is a microcosm of society, and its members represent everyone from the sublime to the ridiculous. The key is in your profile and in your own skills of social filtering, like we do without thinking when we meet new friends or partners in the analogue world.

These filters can be difficult to develop, and I

made many mistakes along the way. Once, I accidently joined an app that might have been Tinder after a friend sent me the link. However, it soon became clear I wasn't in the right place as I got two surprisingly sexual messages from ladies in the first 20 minutes of joining. One of the messages read, "Do you want to kick my back doors in?" Now, imagine being at a bar and that's how a lady introduces herself to you! Besides, as you know, in my eyes, bums are for pooing. And after that colonic irrigation years ago, I am still traumatised. Having brown wings is something I will never want.

Lesson 2: Honesty is the best policy

There was one thing my dates had in common over that two years: they never appeared liked their profiles. I don't know if people think their natural charm on meeting would outweigh the fact they are 10 years older now and four stone heavier. But it doesn't. Regardless of whether age, weight or looks make a difference, if the person you meet in the pub is different to the person you met online, your potential relationship has started with a breach of trust. Frankly, for me, meeting a woman who has presented herself as someone different online is a red flag, a bright warning beacon to not have a second date, no matter how likeable and charming she might be. It is a lie and lies are naughty. So be honest.

Sometimes, the differences can be striking. For instance, I once went on a date with a dwarf. I didn't know she was little prior to meeting; her profile read

5ft 8! That is totally the opposite end of the height spectrum! Also, she didn't have a dwarfy head in her profile picture; you know sometimes dwarves have large heads… But then, perhaps you need to see the whole person for that to show. I asked her why she lied on her description and she said that if she put 3ft 8 she would only attract weirdos. It seemed like the wrong time to mention her two-foot lie made her seem a little weird.

I felt her pain though. People stared at her. I had visions when we were sat in the pub that a waitress would bring over crayons and a colouring book! But then, as my dad used to say, the best things come in small packages. Plus, I imagine she would be a cheap date as she wouldn't eat much!!

There was also a time I met a girl who claimed to work in tourism. I thought maybe she was a holiday rep, but oh no! It turned out she was a bus driver! I suppose you could argue that isn't really a lie, however she also claimed to be 9 stone, but looked like she'd eaten a 9-stone person that morning. Let's just say she probably was that weight in her bra alone! She also said her hobbies included salsa dancing; I think that was a lie too, and she was more into salsa dips!

And there was me thinking the most common lies people say are "I promise", "I love you" and "I'm sorry". Believe me, you will soon learn that people use more lies than those three doing online dating.

Lesson 3: Know what you are looking for in a person

When I first went on dating websites, I believed that finding a partner would be as simple as matching our perfect checklists. In real life, having a mutual love of walking along beaches isn't enough to make you like someone. Can you imagine? *Ahh, you like cats, spontaneous picnics and walking in the rain! You must be the one! Let's ignore the fact the only click we felt was the relief of the door shutting after the first date was finally over.*

Some people take list ticking to a new level and find the oddest of opportunities in online dating matches. I have a female friend who takes it to a completely different level. She doesn't go for blokes for looks or personality, or even for whether they have the same religious views or hobbies. She is interested in what skills they have and what she needs doing to her house. Once, she had a leaky tap and purposely went on a date with a plumber in order to get it fixed free of charge. She is on about replacing her kitchen next year – so if you are a kitchen fitter on Tinder be warned!

It just goes to show women are so much smarter than men. When God created Adam and Eve, I think he took Adam to one side and said, "Look, I have given you two organs. You have a brain, which will allow you create things and have intelligent conversations. And I have given you a penis, which Eve will enjoy and will allow you both to make babies. However, the bad news is you won't be able to use the two organs at the same time!"

But there might be some aspects of list-matching that are useful. Lists don't have to mean things like looks, hobbies, wealth or age. It can mean things you're interested in or desires for the future. For example, I would like to breed one day, so meeting someone who wants kids could save a lot of time and pain dating people who just want to jump my bones. I realise at my age the chances are when I finally meet someone, she will probably already have kids. I don't mind a ready-made family where you just add water, however I would really love a child of my own. Some might argue I need to get a move on as in a few years I might be more in need of the pushchair than any child I can co-create.

Lesson 4: Trust

One of the major downsides to online dating is that it creates trust issues. After a couple of dates, if you like each other, it's probably good advice to take yourselves off the dating site. If you don't it would look like you are keeping your options open, and let's face it, you probably are. Trust is so hard to gain, yet so easy to lose! So, come off the site. If things don't work out, you can always go back. I once met a lovely lady from Street, and to be fair I really wanted to jump her bones, but our date didn't go in that direction. During our friendly, first-meeting chit-chat, she informed me that she had already met someone on the site and had been seeing him for six weeks. She said that as she'd paid for the service, she was keeping her options open! I guess she wanted to get her money's worth!

Chapter 11: The importance of naming

Or, how Profile Names can make or break

your image

Once you have chosen the site you are going to use, you must set up a profile. This can seem like a daunting task and you will have to answer questions you might never have considered, such as how far you are willing to travel for a date, or what colour hair you like. But your profile is all important. It is the first thing your prospective date will meet, and it provides the data for the site to funnel appropriate members towards you.

The first thing people will see along with the thumbnail of your profile picture is your profile name. It is like a slogan to attract people to your full profile. It's strange to think that a combination of a couple of words and possibly a number can say so much; but it's an insight into the soul, or the space where a soul should be…

So, in this chapter I am going to take you through a few of the highs and lows of profile naming.

Lesson 1: Don't give it all away too quickly

Perhaps this stands out to me as I am looking for a relationship and not a hook-up, but I am not convinced that selling your promiscuity in your name is the best way to start out and be treated respectfully. In fact, it can be off-putting to anyone not looking for a quickie. I once had a woman contact me with the name *Legswideopen*. I'm not convinced she was looking for a deep and meaningful relationship. Another innuendo-based name was *Flora* implying she was easy to spread. My female friends assure me men do this too. One friend told me she was contacted by *Hornyforyou*, *WellHung* and *MrGrey* – the final one suggesting he was a stalker as well as looking for kinky sex.

But then, if you're looking for a hook-up, or a fetish encounter, I suppose it makes sense to make that clear from the outset. Perhaps the problem here is that if you are looking for a gang bang, it's probably best to not flirt with someone who is looking for a long-term relationship and quiet walks on a beach. I remember once going on a date with a lady I could describe as Surfboard-Head – I will tell you more about her later – well, she said she had the strangest message from a bloke with the profile name *Tightsniffer*. Before she said anything more, I thought anyone with that as a profile name is going to be a complete nutjob. But then, the story got even more interesting! One of the first things he asked her was whether she was into cuckolding. I had no idea what this meant so she went on to explain that it's when you get invited around to watch a couple have sex... The world is a crazy place!

Lesson 2: Don't be too literal

Since your name should show off something that is best about you, it is important to make it stand out from the thousands of names there. Yet, some people use their own names, which seems a bit boring to me. Others are more creative, and some are just too honest. A lady from Aberdeen has her profile name as *Overweight* – and she wasn't lying. Neither was *TransgenderTerri!*

Country-Girl was another profile name which grabbed my attention since I also live out in the sticks. I thought she might be a suitable match, however after meeting her I thought her profile name should have been *Country-Girl-with-a-Limp*. Apparently, she'd had a terrible horse accident years before and it had left her with wobbly legs. Not that it put me off – I just didn't fancy her anyway.

It's not all bad though. Some include their favourite hobbies in their title, which is possibly a good way to find someone to share those times with. *LoveHolidays* is hard to dislike, for example. *LoveRiding* might have sounded sexual but her pictures showed her horses in the background. But others seem a bit confused, such as *HappyGirl* whose face in her profile picture looked miserable as hell!

RunningGirl was another name that seemed

misplaced – believe me, she didn't look like a runner unless it was to the fridge and back.

Lesson 3: Be original

When you are confronted with lists of names with tiny faces, you need something to attract your attention. Your name is your chance to promote your best attribute or your heart's desire.

Things like favourite colours might seem like a good idea, but don't really work. Besides, colours don't seem to me to be on the list of things it's important for couples to have in common, like religious views, political leanings or approaches to raising children. Have you ever known a divorce happen because a couple couldn't agree on favourite colours? Imagine it now: *I just couldn't take it anymore. His love of yellow was just disgusting. He always ate the yellow sweets, and put daffodils in the garden. Just foul!* Stop and think logically too – there's only so many colours. If you and a million others choose blue as your favourite, how do you stand out? You end up putting the colour followed by a number as the name as already been taken BLUE789, letting everyone know you were the 789th person to think of this.

But you can be too quirky too. Well... perhaps you can't; if you're quirky, perhaps that's exactly the naming style you should use to attract other alternative people to you. After all, someone who calls herself *CosmicConnection* is probably going to be a bit of a hippy. To me, that screams she'll no doubt be a bit do-dally in the head! I'm sure she'd think me a right fuddy-duddy.

There are names that have made me smile though – for good and for bad reasons. *Lovecake* was one of these names; it strikes me as a happy name though I've no idea what she was saying about herself. *DD* was a short and sweet name that drew attention to what I assume she thinks are her greatest assets. There was even a woman on Match called *Chlamydia,* though I'd recommend avoiding her. She probably should have come with a health warning, and some safeguarding team should probably contact her to check she's okay. I also never replied to *Kit-Kat-Kate* as her name sounded so wrong and brought back bad memories of too many fingers...

Some names just don't appear to suit the profile. *TelegramSam* was an obscure name, and I have no idea what it meant – however, her profile made me think she might really be a prostitute using the internet to look for work. *SunflowerCarol* chose a nice twist to her name, however her picture made it look like the weedkiller had got to her. *SunnyGirl* was unfathomably miserable in her picture. An original message I got which made me laugh out loud was from a lady called "Fiery". Her opening line to me was, "I'm looking for a fire starter and you look like an Arsonist." I felt special even tho she probably sent this to every man!!

I have also been contacted by women who use search phrases as their profile names, such as: *Waiting For a Knight in Shining Armour,* and *Are you the one?* Personally, I think women who do this come across a little needy and desperate. I did reply to the *Waiting For a Knight in Shining Armour* lady and told her I only wear jeans and trackies. She did reply, "I'm not looking for a twat in tin foil," which made me smile.

Lesson 4: Numbers are significant

Many people choose to keep things simple and straightforward. Many use their real name followed by important numbers, such as their date of birth. *Tracy86* is a good example. Sometimes, the choice of numbers can be obscure, such as *Michelle225* who messaged me rather a lot. In her case, I can only assume the numbers meant stones! She listed her hobbies as eating! No shit Sherlock! Judging by the pictures, we could have worked this out for ourselves. But then, I'm sure there's lots of people out there looking for their perfect love in someone who loves eating. Relationship Goals, right? I must admit, after attracting a rather lot of big girls, I checked my search criteria to make sure I put age range 30-45 and not in the appearance category under *stones*.

Lesson 5: Some people get really into it

You will be surprised by the amount of people who make contact with you. Some of it – well, most of it – will be unwanted attention that completely ignores what you've said you are interested in. One example of unwanted interest came from a woman who really got into the role of her name.

I'd put on my profile that I wanted someone to settle down and have a family with, so I was a little surprised to get messages from mature ladies. One was a 62-year-old lady. She told me she was a Brownie leader and her interesting fact about herself was she was known as Brown Owl, which she also used as her profile name. She then tried to flirt by asking if I wanted to *ruffle her feathers*! Ruffle was not the word I was looking for! Thank God I had already eaten breakfast that day when that message came through as otherwise I think it would have put me right off.

Genuine profile names

Here are some more examples of people who have contacted me:

Pretzels: Some people put their favourite food as profile name, and I guess this is a friendly and harmless way of introducing yourself. But it does mean you are saying you identify as the food you eat. However, if you are a big girl, names like *ILoveCake* or *CurvyChick* certainly flaunt your assets.

PoshandDirty: Some men might think this sounds like the perfect combination for a lady, however, she didn't look posh! In fact, *BrassyandDominant* might have been a better name judging by the length of her nails, the amount of animal print she was wearing and the long, metal spikes for her heels.

A lot of ladies use inspirational quotes in their profile names. I guess this reveals their state of mind when they decided to jump on the digital bandwagon. *YOLO* (you only live once) was one such lady. She seemed rather nice, but her name made dating sound like a bucket list phenomenon or like she was taking up an extreme sport. Other variations of this type of name were *WhyNotNow* and *OneLifeLiveIt.*

Chapter 12: Profile Information

Or, on TMI, appearing unique and getting to

know you

Once you have your name sorted, it's time for you to complete your full profile. The aim of this is to help prospective dates decide that you are the person they want to contact. Most sites give you a box to fill in that has a character limit. You get to decide what to write – and reading them can tell you a lot about a person. For example, members can reveal they have bitterness or anger issues when they rant, saying things like, *I don't want time wasters, bitches or money grabbers...* Equally, people can show a good sense of humour with funny statements like: *I hear you like bad girls? Well, I'm bad at everything.*

I remember scrolling through loads of ladies' profiles, obviously for research for this book; one rather large lady, in her opening description, put *"Weight Watchers didn't work for me"*, which made me smile. Having the ability to laugh at yourself is a lovely quality. I even saw one terminally ill woman write: *Anyway, I'm dying, so you don't have to worry about a long-term commitment.*

Well, there's not much to say after that!

Your profile is an advert as well as a set of demands. You are aiming to attract interested parties and set out your terms and conditions at the same time. Your demands will largely be ignored; but at least you'll have some defence against any unwanted attention. This can be things like looking for companionship, a long-term relationship, a soul mate... or even, on one profile: *I'm on Tinder to make friends like I'm on Pornhub to learn from a plumber how to fix a sink...* I tend to view free dating sites as sex sites; nobody tends to be looking for serious relationships apart from me, it would seem.

It's a strange phenomenon to advertise yourself like a house for sale. Think about how stressful job applications are to put together, and then imagine that you need to make it hot too! It is no place for polite humility; but arrogance is also off-putting. So, the line to walk is as fine as baby's hair. Easy peasy, then. Like any advert, if it's good it will work well for you. Some people go as far as to say things like: *Hi! I'm Hope, and the P is silent at night...*

So here are my main tips for writing a description: it is almost like going to a swimming pool and seeing the list of what is and isn't allowed in the pool, for example, *No Petting.* Although I haven't drawn you naff diagrams. The one that makes me laugh the most is *No Bombing* with a picture of a black child next to it, which is wrong on so many levels. Just like the swimming pool sign, you will probably ignore most of these points – but they are here for a reason.

Lesson 1: Be yourself!

The main thing is to be real and be yourself. You don't have to be creative or write an autobiography like Michelle Obama's *Becoming*. Often, I think that blokes only look at the pictures anyway. I think women tend to read the details – but then, I wouldn't be able to comment if this were totally true.

You should think of your profile as a chance to promote your best self. In business, there is a process called the "Elevator Pitch", which is a 30-second outline of a new business idea which entrepreneurs use to engage potential investors. The concept is based on the hypothetical situation of being stuck in an elevator for 30 seconds with the boss of a company you wanted to join or enlist; you should think about what is important to know about you, and what qualities you can show. But keep it brief, as I can assure you, nobody will read pages of waffling on.

Lesson 2: Learn from your mistakes and try again!

I have had variable success with my profiles over the years. These are genuinely ones I have used, including two of my least successful attempts.

My first profile read:

I am looking for a lady with the seven Bs: Brains, Beauty, Not on Benefits, able to Breed, No Belly pork, Best friend and not into Bum stuff.

Honestly, I got a fair bit of attention with this one, however it was mainly nutters. I know, many would argue what did I expect with a profile like this!

The funny thing about those who replied to this profile is they were largely mature ladies in their 60s. I'm sure their rivers dried up a long time ago, so they obviously didn't read the breeding part of the seven Bs.

And I'm not sure Maggie99 understood the No Belly Pork bit, as she ran a mobile donut van; judging by her appearance, she probably ate most of what she made.

Please don't think I'm being fattist again. Although I do have a body-weight story that has always made me feel nervous. I guess we could begin with a few stories told to me by a friend who works in a hospital. He told me this story, but he told me others too. The weirdest were things they'd found inside a vagina – bear with me – this does come back to my point, I'm not fattist. He said, the strangest thing they have ever found up a vagina was human poo. Also, a lady once attended A&E with a champagne cork stuck in her flappage; another had a piece of Lego stuck in her. But the worst case, the story that stays with me, was when this large lady entered with stomach pains. Anyway, eventually they looked up her vagina and found a baby's foot! She had soo much belly pork, she didn't even know she was pregnant! Luckily, they managed to turn the baby inside her and she gave birth to a healthy boy. Imagine being that big and not even knowing you were pregnant!?

Anyway, where was I? Oh yes, the seven Bs... I did the best thing I thought I could do and took these comments on board about attracting nutters with this description. I asked a female friend to write me a sensible one, which I then added for 36 hours. It wasn't long. You'll see why. It went along the lines of:

Funny guy with a great sense of humour; sporty, kind and caring. It carried on, but listing good qualities in a non-personal way, with nothing specific.

I had zero response from this; zero!

My third example summed me up more. Again, this is a genuine profile:

Lonely old Mountain Goat with Big Horn seeks female Love Goat – doesn't have to have big teats or a bell around her neck, however just someone to share my mountain with.

This heralded a lot of attention and some lovely dates. I didn't need to say I had a good sense of humour, I just needed to show it. I also didn't need to say I was romantic, but I could reveal it.

Lesson 3: Don't give instructions!

Instructions can make you sound closed minded at best and controlling at worst. Who wants to follow an instruction from a stranger? Who wants criteria to meet to attract a date? For most of us, we want to meet someone who is genuinely attracted to us, and not based on specific preliminary changes. If you don't like what you see, then move on to the next profile. Don't use your profile to insult people before you even begin.

One guy on Tinder has taken a roasting in the press for using his profile to tell women how to be more feminine. Now, you might like a lady who is well made up – or you might be one, but I'm not sure telling a woman to make more of an effort is the best way to start a conversation. Unless you want that conversation to be angry.

Equally, telling people to not contact you if they're a douchebag is not going to work. It makes you sound bitter and will probably attract douchebags who will tell you so.

It also makes me laugh the number of times blokes will slag off an ex-girlfriend on the description. I've seen things like, 'I'm looking for someone who is nothing like my ex…' Just don't do it; move on with dignity. An ex is an ex for a reason, and she or he deserves to have a chance to date again themselves. Besides, we should never bring up exes in conversations with potential dates.

Lesson 4: Have fun!

I have used business analogies above, which are great at showing how you need to make an impression precisely and quickly. But I certainly don't mean for you to take away a formal and ambitious approach to dating. Lurrve is meant to be thrilling in the beginning, filled with love and memories as it develops. Life is tough and relationships are hard work, so you need the good, juicy, yummy stuff to keep you going. Your profile should show a bit of your flavour.

It's also fun to use metaphors, like my mountain goat. Who doesn't feel warm and snuggly when anthropomorphising their lives? And yes, I did have to look up that word.

Lesson 5: Don't point your flaws or health issues

We all have flaws, be it a wonky nose, lazy eye, or missing limb – there is no need to point this bit out in your description. Yes, I do think having the ability to laugh at yourself is an amazing quality, but your profile description is designed to sell yourself. Believe me, people will take note of everything you have written about yourself.

Chapter 13: Profile Pictures

Or, on selfies and saying cheese

I've no idea how soooooo many people get this bit so wrong… Surely, it's just a case of uploading a picture of yourself that looks as attractive as you can. Somehow, a significant proportion of dating site members confuse this simple requirement. I'm not sure if they just don't know what they look like or can't see their own face in 2D: whichever way, their ability to choose between versions of their own face is seriously flawed.

Humans have developed sophisticated languages, complex cultures and advanced technologies – tech so advanced it can take accurate pictures of your face, and yet somehow there are humans who cannot choose a good likeness to present their face to the world.

There are only a few requirements, one of which is that it is preferable to be smiling. It really is as simple as that. A smile is the most powerful communication there is; a smile is so powerful that you can walk past someone in the street, smile at them and the chances are they will smile back. This is unless you live in London where a smile might get you stabbed for being sarcastic. There is a saying that you are not fully dressed until you wear a smile – I believe this to be true like I believe my dad's wisdom. Obviously, you still need clothes as well... A smile says a lot about a person so it's important to have a picture of you beaming away! Obviously, if you only have three teeth you can smile with your mouth closed – if you wish. If you have a mouth like a horse, I would probably do the same as there are ivory poachers everywhere these days.

It always cracks me up how so many people just look utterly miserable in their profile pictures. I can't accurately count the amount of times I've looked at pictures and thought, *God! Serial killer!* And the ones with roller-coaster faces put a smile on my face too!

Lesson 1: Choose a good picture of you, but be aware others might choose badly for themselves!

For some people, looks are everything! It is true that blokes scroll through ladies available online via their pictures first; it is also true they will rule them out without looking into their profiles if they don't like what they see. Therefore, it is also true blokes can be complete losers for doing this. Apparently, ladies are the complete opposite: they read through profiles and the picture is of secondary importance. Perhaps women are better at realising the picture doesn't say it all – especially if the bloke can't choose an image that looks like his own face! Of course, some might argue blokes are just being more efficient when it comes to online dating. I never noticed how different men and women just are until one day I noticed parents dropping off their kids to school: if a dad is dropping off his child, he gets to the school gates, drops the child off and goes. But women use this time for mum-chat and small talk. "My little Charlie has just started swimming lessons… blah, blah, blah!" Cripes! They are there for ages! So, no wonder they delve into everything on your profiles! Blokes just keep it simple; one look at the picture and they move on. Anyway, where was I?

Despite the poor-quality images that are frequently selected and the foolishness of judging someone solely on their looks, I'm not about to tell you to abandon the profile picture; you have to be attracted to someone, so fancying them in the first instance is handy. However, you must remember not everyone is photogenic and a picture will only tell you so much.

Besides, from my experience, the ladies that have the most beautiful appearance on the outside normally have the ugliest or dullest of personalities. I'm sure that's true in return. Thank God for my lazy eye!

Lesson 2: Have a variety of pictures

In an ideal world, you should post a few pictures and ensure there is a variety of shots. You know, when we look to buy a house you want images of different angles and different rooms. Not saying that you're as fat as a house, though you might be. You should perhaps include at least one head shot and one a full-length shot. As a rule, and from experience, I would never date a girl (again) who just has a head shot. You might call it shallow, but I don't want to waste anyone's time. And I certainly don't want to be rude to someone when we could have avoided the awkwardness. I mean, some people might have pretty heads, but Oh! My! God! There was a reason why they didn't show the rest of their features! This is normally because they are on the sea food diet. Sorry, I mean, SEE food diet. Although I'm not sure they wait long enough to see the food before they eat it! It was a bit of a running joke between my friends and I for a while regarding the fact I seem to attract the larger lady. At one stage, I considered getting a bigger vehicle as I'm sure my van had a weight limit.

Lesson 3: Eyes are windows to a response

It might seem obvious but avoid wearing sunglasses. I must admit, I have been guilty of this as, believe it or not, due to my wonky eye I have never been comfortable having my picture taken. But as a rule of thumb (as if thumbs had rules in the first place) whatever is covered up in a profile picture is hidden for a reason.

However, the timeless romantic rule continues: we all want to gaze lovingly into someone's eyes. The profile picture is the first chance to prove your eyes are gaze-worthy. You might think you look cool wearing shades, but you'll just end up looking shady. So crack out your peepers and invite the love in!

Lesson 4: Be honest!

I have heard so many horror stories of people meeting someone who was barely recognisable from their profile picture. I don't know how someone thinks putting pictures that were taken when they were ten years younger is going to work out – as if walking into a bar and meeting someone who might be the parent of the person you were expecting is seductive and charming… If you are serious about meeting someone, don't be a dick! It's as simple as that!

Put a recent picture – and when I say recent, make sure it is no older than six months as it will be obvious, and it is off-putting. Both men and women are guilty of this, despite the fact it is a pointless bluff. How does someone think their personality will be striking enough to charm someone over after the first impression they have given is one of deceit?

I never really understood why anyone would do this; surely, when you meet in person it's hard to hide the disappointment of them not being what you expected. I have had this happen so many times!

Lesson 5: Don't hide behind your friends

Over the years, I have noticed many ladies have pictures of them with their friends as their profile pictures. I have never understood this as it can cause confusion; after all, why would you want to attract a potential partner to your friend? However, it seems to always work just one way. So, don't be fooled; if you are having difficulty working out which one the lady is, you can guarantee she will be the ugly one! Without a doubt!

Lesson 6: Use Photoshop at your peril

With all of modern technology available at the touch of a fingertip, people can filter their pictures. This is called catfishing. The term was first used in the 2010 documentary 'Catfish', in which Nev Schulman discovered the gorgeous woman he fell in love with online was a actually a middle-aged, married mum and not the 25-year-old he was led to believe. It could be perceived as a judgement of the middle-aged woman; in reality, Schulman was duped into developing feelings for a person who didn't exist.

I don't get why you would filter your picture. I recall a date I had with a girl from Totnes who appeared nothing like her profile picture. In real life you know when you get an oil spill at sea, well her face looked a bit like that. It was all patchy, minus the seagulls covered in oil of course!

On social media, so many people these days add filters to their pictures; these can be harmless, such as funny ears or glasses. That's fine for Facebook, but it isn't for online dating. Going back to my house analogy, you'd be pretty peed off if you went to see a renovated three-bed semi and discovered it was a two-bed with the damp hidden behind paintings. It would be equally disappointing if you found it was really detached with large out-buildings and was going for £50k more than you'd budgeted. Remember, not everyone is going to like your online dating picture and that is okay. You're not looking for laughs so back the truck up, buddy, and drop the bunny ears and over-sized eyes. Equally, it's not like when you post a new profile picture on Facebook and you wait all smug with anticipation to see how many likes you get. You need to deal with the fact not everyone is going to fancy you, and your mum and Aunt Kathy aren't there to tell you you're beautiful anyway.

Deal with it.

Lesson 7: SpongeBob SquarePants does not have the strangest head shape in the world...

This next anecdote might sound like I've made it up; I swear I haven't. I swear it on the lives of Pjork and Kevin Bacon, my beloved pet pigs. I've genuinely been on dates with ladies who have profile pictures of them with normal shaped heads, yet when I met them in real life they have different shaped heads. It had never occurred to me before online dating that head shape can be important, but I have subsequently found out it really is!

One particular time I remember, I met a girl in Yeovil who had a really long face. It had been fine in her profile picture but in the flesh it looked like a surfboard. I mentioned her head looked a little different and she openly admitted she had doctored the picture. I might not have noticed had I just met her at a bar like meeting someone in the olden times; but as she'd promoted herself as having a regular, oval shaped head, the long ironing board came as a surprise!

Just don't do it! If you have a long face like a horse, keep it real! Some bloke will like you, and not because he wants to enter you into the Grand National! And we are not talking about entering from behind! I truly believe there is someone out there for everyone, and despite my jokes, we're all drawn to different shapes and sizes, so wear your size and shape with pride. If I don't fancy you, you might just consider yourself lucky! And vice versa! Besides, it's freak or unique: the chances are your picture will stand out if you do look a bit different.

Lesson 8: Over-compensation isn't cool

A lot of ladies post pictures of themselves on holidays and in their bikinis; while this might appeal to many men, I'm not convinced it's the best way to attract the right attention. But then, I don't actually know what attention you want, so maybe it is. In my eyes, however, less is more – and I mean less having it all on show and not less clothing.

Blokes often do the same thing; they post a picture of themselves with tanned bodies and six packs. But if you just concentrate on showing off your body, it strikes me that you're over-compensating for something else that is missing. Get your mind out of the gutter again! Sadly, this is often a personality.

Looks only get you so far in life; when I was a kid there was a really good-looking bloke in my town, but I was always aware he wasn't taken very seriously. This was because his nickname was Trigger: he might have had the looks, but he was thick as shit and had the brains of a rocking horse and as my dad would say, "Not the sort you'd want on your pub quiz team."

I guess if you need to undress to impress you are missing something in life. I think it's the same as when people post pictures of themselves next to expensive things; a way to look good when there's nothing else good going on. It's like the age-old cliché when men post pictures of themselves next to big flashy cars; they might as well use the profile name TinyPenis.

Lesson 9: The background matters

You need to be so conscious of your profile picture background because believe me people do take notice! I had a 72-year-old lady contact me who had a mobility scooter in the background of her picture; I'm not being funny, but if she's struggling to walk now, she doesn't have a chance with a stallion like me!

A lot of ladies take pictures in their bedrooms in front of a full-length mirror; again you can tell a lot of the lady by the tidiness and things in a room. God! I have seen some pictures where women have clothes scattered all over the floor, including underwear and onesies… None of these things are terrible, but it might be too soon to know that your guilty collection is unicorn undies, or even worse underwear on the floor that only your gran would wear: gurt apple catchers. In one picture, I swear I saw what looked like a vibrator on the side of her bedside cabinet. Ordinarily that shouldn't be a problem – a little soon, perhaps, but not a problem. But I didn't contact her purely because of the size of the dildo! I thought she must have some kind of bucket in her pants! I was worried If I ever entered her, I would disappear like a plane flying through the Bermuda Triangle! I don't typically feel inadequate in the trouser snake department, but Oh! My! That would make my arm look small!

Other things I have noticed in the background of profile pictures include wedding photos, which is really personal. Once there was a lollypop stick complete with high-viz jacket on the floor. I then drove past a lollypop lady the other day and did a double-take; that can't be a good sign!

Probably the most common thing I see in the background is the a 'NotOnTheHighStreet' style sign of 'Live, Laugh, Love'. Call me cynical, but if you need to be reminded to do these things each day, there is no hope! But then, I do like the saying 'grinners are winners', so I suppose each to their own. I don't have it framed on my bedroom wall though.

Lesson 10: Your pets are not as cute to strangers

It's also common for ladies to post pictures of their pets, be it horses, cats, dogs or many other cute and cuddly pets. I know we find it hard to resist a cat meme or videos of ducks riding on ponies or dogs in socks on YouTube. But I'm not on a dating site to be entertained by animal humour or to check out your pussy! At best your pets will be ignored; at worst you'll be contacted by someone who is more interested in your pets than you! Can you imagine that? Having to put up with a date who's only interested in riding your pony…

One lady I spoke to even had a picture of her goldfish! I'm not sure what she was saying about herself with that picture other than she was remarkably good at keeping something so vulnerable alive! It's an interesting fact that about 30% of pet owners let their pets sleep on the bed with them. I'm hoping the lady with the goldfish didn't sleep with hers, but it does show how close we are with our pets. Mine taught me how to love; but I'm not sure I want him on a date with me. I want to get to know a woman without her fawning over the softness of Smirnoff's fur. Anyway, my point is I'm just not convinced profile pictures should be of your pets.

I guess women are making it clear they have animals and if you're not a cat lover there's no point getting in contact. I think it is strange why ladies love cats so much; after all, they are independent, they don't listen, they don't come in when your call, they stay out all night, and when they are home they like to be left alone to sleep. In other words, every quality that women hate in men they love in cats!

Anyway, where was I? Your profile picture should be of you, not of things to attract attention because a man or woman might like those things irrespective of you. One woman even posted a picture of a cake she made; did she expect a guy to be like oh! I love cake so this must be the lady for me? I'm not being funny, if you believe the quickest way to a man's heart is the stomach, you know you are aiming a little too high...

Lesson 11: Food glorious food!

Talking of food, the amount of ladies who post pictures of them with something in their mouths also cracks me up. I don't mean them being seductive with a banana or licking an ice cream, which might also give a specific impression. I think the worst ones are when the lady is overweight and she is pictured eating. I think we can tell already that eating is one of your favourite hobbies; don't over-egg that pudding!

At the end of the profile setting-up, everyone wants their picture to look the best it possibly can. I guess we're all trying to make sure the right angle obstructs any birth marks or other flaws of which we are conscious. I guess the point I'm trying to make is just be true to yourself. You'll be drawn to certain people, like I am. And others will put you off. And there'll be plenty of people interested in you too. If you do have a huge nose, don't hide it! As my dad always says, the truth will always come out. And besides, Postman Pat had a massive hooter and even he managed to find a wife.

Chapter 14: Lies

Lies and Randomness

In my obviously humble opinion, lying is the worst of the issues in online dating. It comes up time and again across my chapters in one guise or another; it is a problem committed by far too many members; it always gets discovered, thereby making those members seem like idiots at best and untrustworthy or frightening at worst. Yet it is more virulent than the clap in my home town.

I have never understood why people lie. It seems such a strange thing to lure a date with photos from a decade ago, as if the lighting in any bar is going to delete 10 years of aging – and eating. Worst still are the Photoshoppers; slimming arms, thighs, and even faces to make them look not only better but totally different. So different it is easy to walk past them as if you've never seen them before. In many respects, you haven't. One would think the days of wearing a pink carnation to recognise your date are gone, but prolific photo editing has made it as hard to recognise a new date as it is to match the adult Michael Jackson to his childhood photos.

When writing your profile, just be yourself. If you are serious about meeting someone, don't try to be someone you are not as you won't get more than one date. If someone likes you they will accept all your flaws. So if you are 19 stone, don't put 9 stone and claim it must be a typo error when you meet. If you are 3 foot 8 don't put 5 foot 8. If you are serious about meeting someone, honesty is the best policy. Okay, so I didn't mention the fact I have a lazy eye in his profile description, but you can kind of see it in some pictures (it's not apparent all of the time). But it did make someone smile from reading my full profile; and I have heard it said that if you can make a girl laugh, you are halfway there.

So let me take you through a range of liars, from the sublime to the mental. Some of these women were genuinely lovely and attractive, but starting a first date with a lie is an automatic no for me. It probably should be for you too. One female friend of mine overlooked a confessed lie about age on the first date, and she ended up with a stalker. Just saying.

1. Be honest about what you are looking for

Perhaps unrelatedly, but I went through a stage of going on dates with women I call GLOBS: Good Looking Old Birds. I have never like the term MILF, and GLOB is so much more satisfying to say. I met this one lady who was 47 years old after we hit it off online. We'd chatted for a while and she seemed interesting. We arranged our first date to be for daytime coffee as this seem to be the norm when meeting a mature lady; I'm guessing at night-time they are home in front of the TV with a blanket over their knees.

Now, I have to confess, she was stunning; I'd be lying if I said I didn't want to jump her bones. But I had to stay strong as I discovered she was a double liar! The thing that put me right off was when she told me she had already met someone from the dating site and that they had been together nearly six weeks. I felt like she was properly wasting my time, yet she acted as though she was shopping around to see if she could get a better deal. I felt so sorry for the unwitting guy who thought he was six weeks into something good. Apparently, she thought it was justifiable as she had already paid for 6 months subscription – she wanted to get her money's worth!

2. Don't hide disabilities

It might be a dodgy topic, but I genuinely don't think you should advertise yourself as 'perfect'. We all have flaws and sometimes disabilities should be acknowledged as normally as your hair colour. It's not just to ensure your potential date isn't put off, but to also ensure they don't respond in shock or surprise.

In my experience, surprise was a part of the problem – and then I felt like an arse for bringing it up and discussing it. It all happened when I went on a date with a girl with the profile name Country-Girl. She seemed perfect – as I live out in the sticks now, I thought our lifestyles might align. She was a little younger than me at 29, but in my romantic mind I thought this might be perfect as I wanted to breed in the future. However, we didn't gel that well.

But her profile name should have been Country-Girl-With-a-Limp. Now – it might not seem so important, and her disability probably wasn't for life. But typically when anyone has just had a serious accident, don't we mention it in conversation? You know, we'd spent hours chatting by message and then on the phone. You'd have thought she'd have mentioned her leg aching or physio appointments or something. But no. Instead, the first I knew of it was when we tried to walk into the bar and she walked as if one leg belonged to someone else. And I felt like a right twat trying to pretend like everything was normal.

When we eventually tackled the lame elephant in the corner of the room, it turned out she had recently had a serious horse-riding accident and now walked funny.

And then I was just left feeling shallow for not wanting to see her again – should I have said it isn't because of her leg? It was more to do with the fact I thought it was weird she hadn't mentioned it… and the fact I am just not as country as I thought.

3. Be proud of what you do and who you are

Once, I even ended up going on a date with a bus driver. No – not a 50-year-old man with a beer belly, but a female bus driver. Not that there's anything wrong with being a 50-year-old man with a beer belly – some of them are my friends. I don't want to date them though. My date, however, was a female bus driver. Yet, she didn't put that in her job description; instead, it said she worked in tourism. Now, I realise people upsell themselves all the time, and I guess working in tourism is kind of true. And I'm not sure why it matters, except it is a deception.

But with this bus driving tour operator continued the deceptions. In her photo she looked slim, attractive and her hobbies included salsa dancing. Naively, I thought she'd be fit and active. And I stupidly expected her to look like her photo, something I will come onto shortly. Now, when I first met her, I thought she must have meant salsa dips with copious amounts of chips as she was a lot bigger than I was expecting. Then she gave the standard excuse – the picture was a few years old, and she just didn't have many photos. Besides, it shouldn't be about the size but about the person... And she was right – but only to some extent. I felt like I'd been taken for a fool, and she was deluding herself. Why would she want a man who fancies a woman by a totally different description? I thought, it would have been nice to know in advance she had a loyalty card for Greggs, as after all I had clearly put on my list I was looking for someone with no belly pork!

4. Use a photo of yourself, Goddammit!

The very first online date I ever went on sort of set the tone for all the bad dating online disasters I have had since. In my experience, almost none of the ladies have ever looked like their profile pictures or have been anything like how they describe themselves. Nowadays, I'm inclined to just not bother working out who the photo fits most closely in the bar I enter. If the photo is not of you now, I don't want the date.

I was seriously nervous for my first date. I had chatted a few times to the lady in question on the phone before meeting, and we got on well, so I was optimistic and full of butterflies. However, that illusion was soon to be shattered. I spruced myself up, put on my lucky pants, and drove to the pub she suggested for us to meet. On reflection, perhaps my lucky pants are not my lucky pants at all!

In my defence, she claimed to be slim in her profile. Let's just say she was a size Mark F, which is one up on a Marque! I don't have anything against fat people, but she was more than double the woman I was expecting to meet! I learnt a valuable lesson that day: if a lady has only used a headshot as a profile picture, there is probably a good reason why!

Can you believe, she even suggested coming back to my house after the date? I was thinking, *Well, I don't have a lot of food in the house, so she might eat one of the cats!*

I know concentrating on looks is superficial, but it's the first point you start with when you meet online, and photos are the visual evidence you are meant to be able to trust. But you really can't rely on these images. Another girl I met from Yeovil seemed pleasant to chat to, but again, photo deception really put me off. When we met, I couldn't help notice that her head was lot thinner and longer than her profile picture. After noticing I was looking at her intently, she confessed that she altered her pictures a little bit.

In fairness, I felt a bit sorry for her. She told me on the date that most blokes who contact her are odd balls and send pictures of their *anatomy* etc. She said the sweetest message she had was from a bloke who wanted to meet her in KFC, and his words to her were, "I'll pay and treat you."

She turned it down.

But that was her best offer. Things online are not good.

5. Another picture point – keep them up to date!

It's a shame but I think it might be true – the longer you are single, the more barriers you tend to put up when you meet people. It's easy to become so jaded that it can be just the smallest detail which can put you off. The downside to this is the higher you build the walls around your heart, the harder you fall when someone tears them down. But you have to get to that first, and it's impossible when people keep doing the oddest of things.

I have learnt to not to focus on the negatives and more on the positives – but this is seriously tested at times. Such as when I met a vet who looked nothing like her profile picture but more like a ferret. Awkwardly, she asked me what my first impression of her was. Honest to the last, I blurted out, "Well, you look nothing like what I was expecting..." She replied that she had used an old picture to lure men in. LURE MEN IN! Like some kind of praying mantis! I imagined her with sticky tentacles reaching out to take me captive. What a response! I thought, that might lure them in, but I bet none of them stick around. She then confirmed this: she said she had no problem finding men, just keeping them. I thought, if you are going to mislead a bloke, what do you expect?

6. The children question

I couldn't get my head around why nobody told the truth on these sites, but I wasn't about to start accepting the lies. So on my way home I sent her a pre-saved text I'd prepared for such moments: Thanks for a nice date, don't see it going anywhere – wish you all the best in the future.

This just happened to be the same text I sent after meeting a 40-year-old from Exmouth a few weeks later. She looked amazing in her picture and she had it all going on like a leg a lamb. She was the right age range for me as I didn't want to go out with anyone under thirty, and I certainly didn't want to go out with anyone much older than 40 as in the back of my mind I still wanted to find a breeding partner. So when Mavis who was 68 kept contacting me, it was pointless replying as she would have been drier than a camel's nostrils in a desert storm!

Anyway, back to the Exmouth lady; after chatting briefly online we arranged to meet up quite quickly. We were both fairly excited that they had found each other and seem to tick so many boxes. But oh my god how wrong I was! The first bombshell happened when I picked her up from her house, which is not the norm on a first date and I would certainly not recommend to anyone; meet in a neutral place for safety! She was wearing these big leather boots that went all the way to her thigh; I genuinely thought she was on the game. I know you women are like walking theme parks with so many bits and bobs to play with, however I'd rather be with a women like Wookey Hole where not many people visit, than Alton Towers where everyone has had a ride!

The next bombshell happened over the first drink. To her credit she told me straight away after meeting, but I think it was the kind of information that should have been revealed in our early chats. "I've lied on my profile," she sheepishly confessed. I thought, *Here we go,* and fixed a polite smile on my face. "I have five kids," she blurted out. Again, I recall her profile description as specifically stating she did not have any and would like children one day! The date didn't last long after that. Again, she said that she didn't mention in her profile that she had kids in fear of putting men off. I told her it was more the fact that she had lied and not because she had spent most of her life on her back… giving birth if nothing else. She was also keen to show off her trumpet blowing skills on a first date, she didn't even own a trumpet!

7. It's not just dating websites where we should be mindful of lies

Strangely, while online dating I set myself an age limit. I mentioned 30 to 40, but I vowed to myself privately I wouldn't go below 25 years old or over 45.

However, I can honestly say that I never stuck to these rules in real life. I suppose it is because dating websites press you to put something in the age boxes.

One particular date stands out; we met after she befriended me on Facebook. I didn't have a Scooby Doo who she was, however, she was incredibly fit, so I thought what the hell! Just accept! I must admit, if she had looked like a back of end of a bus, I wouldn't have been so willing. I really need to rethink my online safety strategy.

After a few days, she posted a selfie of herself online. It was a lovely picture, and being a typical single bloke, I liked it. This led to us striking up a conversation. Now, she was nearly 18 years younger than me. I was 41 and she was 23… And I must admit, I quite liked the attention she was giving me. However, being a realist, I knew it wasn't going to lead to anything. At that stage I thought it might be just a bit of harmless banter on social media. But, unusually, it led to a date.

She was a nurse, and I don't mind openly admitting part of me thought it could be handy later on in life: instead of paying for a full time carer, I'd have a younger nurse performing my bedside duties.

But things didn't go according to any kind of plan. We arranged to meet a few times, however at last minute she would always back out and have an excuse as to why she was cancelling. I just thought it served me right: young girls just play games and love the attention, and I'd been suckered in. However, when I started to ignore her, she quickly got back in contact and arranged another date.

The evening came and we met in a secluded car park in Sidmouth – I promise this was her idea. We met quite late, it was 9pm. I wasn't nervous to be fair; on the night I half expected her to not turn up due to her mucking me around previously. But she did, and I almost wished she hadn't. She looked quite classy in her pictures online, so I knew she wouldn't turn up in roller skates or wearing a bum bag like girls my age had back in the day. But then, what can I honestly say considering she might read this one day... Even though it was dark, I could tell she looked nothing like her Facebook pictures. She had a chin like Jimmy Hill. To say I was disappointed was an understatement. She also sounded like she was on drugs as she was almost away with the fairies. And the whole conversation we had was about everything that she had wrong with her. I'm sure it would have been easier to ask what she had right with her. I tried to show sympathy and respect, however either she is a medical mystery or someone who wants people to feel sorry for her. I'm not quite sure how much I believed she had wrong with her, as it seemed such a weird date introduction.

I realised quite late my main question should have been, did she get hit by a bus before she arrived? She didn't resemble her pictures. Once over the health bamboozlement, I asked her, to which she replied, "I did a bit of catfishing."

I was like, "Sorry, what does that mean?"

She replied, "A bit of filtering."

No shit, Sherlock! I thought! Even though I have a theory that ladies with wonky noses are better snoggers, there was no chance she was getting any kind of kiss from me. Her frigging chin was soooo big you wouldn't be able to get close to her lips unless you went in sideways!

Chapter 15: Making Contact

Or, on Winking, Waving and Which Way to

Swipe

So, once you have selected your best pictures and written your profile, you are ready to see who is out there and looking for love – like you. You'll have obviously taken all my advice, and your pictures will be smiling, and will not include lots of animals or other people's children. Your profile will be warm and engaging, full of your own personal wit and charm.

But the effort doesn't stop there. Sorry.

There are a few ways of navigating the next step, which is to contact people who you might like to speak to more. You might know you fancy them, or their profile might have caught your attention. One way to contact them is to do a search for the type of person you are looking for; or you can chat to people who are currently online when you are. The safer option is the latter as old profiles are kept on these sites, so you don't know if they are still active members. But then, is dating about playing safe?

Lesson 1: Winking is no longer weird

You'll probably feel a little shy to begin with as you get to grips with the site. So, let me clue you in to some of the obvious features. There's an easy way to reach out to grab someone's attention without sending a message straight off. A lot of the sites have a Wink feature... I know, right? In real life, standing in a bar and winking at people to indicate you are interested in them might get you a few stares at best, and a drink over you at worst. But online winking is a good thing. It's not even a sign of a nervous twitch.

I believe winking is intended to cushion you from too much rejection – as if a non-returned wink is easier to overcome than an ignored message. Perhaps it is. Though probably an instruction to change your hair, or how you should dress is worse than both of these. But winking is a good thing. Messages might be hard to keep up with if you're being gregarious, whereas you can wink away at tons of folk with no stress at all.

Though it does get weird if you just keep winking at someone. I once heard from a woman who returned winks with a guy seven times each before one of them sent a message. I think she wondered whether he was sending a message in Morse code. Perhaps he wanted saving from a difficult situation... But then, I also wonder why she didn't send him a message either.

Joking aside, they did end up dating for a few months, so it didn't do any harm.

You will get a lot of winks. People do this to see if you are interested in them, cautiously gauging keenness; but be careful to not wink at everyone and anyone – even if you are a naturally friendly person. To begin with, my friendliness definitely caused me some grief… In my early days, in a happy manner, I returned winks to two women, Sharon, who was 61 years old, and Fat-Pat (her self-appointed name) aged 71. I just thought they were being friendly. Subsequently, they kept winking at me every day. They're probably still winking at my dormant profile now!

Lesson 2: Get out from behind your digital eyelids

Personally, I think winking is pointless and shows lack of personality. Once you've got the hang of the site and you're happy with your profile, just drop someone a line and say hello. If they like the look of you, they will reply. If they don't reply, you haven't lost anything. And at least you're not going to end up in a wink-off with someone who's just being friendly and doesn't know how to let you down.

Though, it is important to note: don't make the mistake I made at the start and reply to everyone out of politeness. It will not do you any favours. It might create a weirdly traumatic experience for you. People on dating sites are not there to just be friendly (unless of course their profile says they're there to just make friends). The aforementioned Fat-Pat got the wrong end of the stick and thought I wanted a bit of GILF (gran I'd love to f@ck).

Lesson 3: Hello!

In my experience, the opening line of your initial message needs to grab the recipient's attention. I spent 12 years working in radio so I can be pretty creative; I've always thought I would be brilliant on the old 80s TV show, Catchphrase, as I often just say what I see! And this can be good advice on a dating site too. Don't go for the obvious and the cliched, such as, "Phwoar! You look beautiful!" It's cheesy and insincere, even if she or he is really good-looking. Instead, single out a feature; if she has a great forehead, tell her. It shows creativity and will put a smile on her face. Plus, she might never have had a compliment like that before.

In the early days of online dating I so got it wrong on many occasions; my opening line to Kirsty9 was one of those times, where my opening line was, *'Is Kirsy9 code word for K9? Cos you don't look like a dog.'* Apparently, Kirsty did not like this.

Lesson 4: Get to know your potential date

Once you strike up a conversation, get to know him or her. This might seem obvious, but it's easy to get stuck in a superficial and polite chat that doesn't go anywhere. Asking questions is logical, but you don't have to go for the predictable ones, such as: what job do you do? Do you have any pets? Or, how long have you been single? It might be good to avoid questions about star signs too, although if you're a guy and you're chatting to a girl, in my experience there's a high chance she's going to crack that one out at you shortly anyway.

If you can get creative with your questions, not only will you find out about your potential date's personality, but other conversations will open too. You must also read through the lady's profile and ask her lots of questions about herself; it shows you are genuinely interested in her and that you have taken time to start getting to know her. You can also be more playful with your questions and ask things like: what actor/actress would they choose to play them in a movie based on their life; what super-power would they choose if they could have one; what would be their survival strategy if a zombie apocalypse began tomorrow; or even what five things would they want with them if they were stranded on a desert island.

Don't ask whether they voted Brexit or remain – unless you're desperate to use a Russian Roulette approach to conversation starting.

The main thing is to be sincere and if you are genuine, you'll ask open ended questions in order to get to know that person. Don't talk just about yourself, how much you earn, or what you have got. Life and love is never about how much you've got; it's always way more about who you have got. Plus, there's a fine line between peacocking and just blatant arrogance – nobody loves a trumpet blower.

Lesson 5: Online dating is a multi-dating space

In real life, typically flirting and dating is a long building process; it often starts within a community, so we build up from smiling at each other, through the butterflies stage, to rutting beasts, all with one person. Online, however, the chances are your potential date will be in contact with loads of people. As will you too.

This is exciting as there's so many people to meet. But it has its challenges. Firstly, like social media, online dating can become a time-consuming thing. While everyone around you is scrolling Facebook and adding likes, you'll find yourself swiping left and right, and replying to winks, and the next thing you know you'll have missed the latest episode of Game of Thrones. Joffrey forbid!

Additionally, you can run the risk of getting potential dates confused. Check your messages carefully; always look at the profile information to be sure; and don't have too many potential dates on the go at the same time. Unlike one of my friends who agreed to meet one guy she was really interested in, only to have the guy she wasn't particularly interested in turn up. She'd sent the '*sorry but I'm not interested*' message to the wrong man. To make matters worse, she then tried to message him to explain, but funnily enough he didn't reply again.

I used to have a golden rule, I would focus on getting to know one girl at a time and once we had arranged a date to meet up, would start chatting to another – now this might seem shallow however I was planning on getting my money's worth. Plus, I had such low expectations when meeting potential dates I had another one lined up and in the bag. I always wanted a win-win situation; when one door closes another one opens…

Lesson 6: Get offline and speak in real life

There's obviously no need to rush things when you meet someone online; after all, you are beginning to know someone who was a complete stranger with perhaps no shared friends to help build trust and to have some common ground. But, if you're interested in them, I think it's important to get speaking at least on the phone sooner rather than later.

A lot of women will ask for your full name so they can check you out on Facebook. I have agreed to this a couple of times, but to my peril! Now, I would avoid this at all costs, as some nutjobs have gone through everything on my Facebook analysing and commenting on private family stuff. Worse is when they then start asking questions about pictures they have seen on your Facebook profile. Everyone has a past, and the downside with social media is it constantly gets dragged back up.

When you get a phone number, call them and talk in person, and you'll soon know whether you click with them or not. You will learn more in five minutes of speaking with someone or meeting them in person than you could from sending a thousand emails to each other. People craft their emails, and get friends to help them reply. But when you're speaking on the phone, you will know whether you're conversation builds organically. If someone who can craft a romantic and poetic email can't keep sentences flowing from their mouth, you'll know he or she had some help.

Obviously, if you are nervous about talking on the phone for the first time, write down some bullet points of things to ask. Don't talk about the weather as a conversation opener if you can help it. The number of people who do this is astonishing; when I worked in radio we had a rule that we were not allowed to mention the weather in the first 10 minutes of conversation each day. Check it out – you will notice at your workplace how most people will comment on the weather as the first thing they say each day. People constantly use clichés and bland, obvious statements such as, *'God, it's cold!'* or, *'What a lovely morning.'*

Lesson 7: Online love can't go the distance

This might sound strange to some, however, there is no point contacting ladies who are more than 50 miles away from where you live – online daters don't want to travel too far – all those rubbish quotes about distance is just a test to see how far your love can travel is nonsense. I have bucked this trend only twice where I travelled to Manchester and London to meet different ladies. Both dates were disasters. Plus, since I had travelled so far, I felt obliged to spend the day with them.

The Manchester lady, who claimed to be looking for a prince as she described herself as a *Disney Land Princess*, was a real surprise. She was more like the Poundland princess, and it was clear on arrival she was keen on getting some Real Devon Ambrosia inside her – honestly, I will tell you about it.

She picked me up from the train station in Manchester and the journey had taken best part of four hours. Just before arriving at the platform, I freshened up, sprayed on a bit of aftershave and looked forward to meeting this so called *Disney Land Princess*. What greeted me on Platform 3 I can only describe as *BoBFoC* (Body off Baywatch, Face off Crimewatch). She was not the sweet, innocent Snow White she made herself out to be either; this was evident when we went to her house for a drink. Please bear in mind this was the first time we had met in person, though we had previously spoken a few times on the phone. She told me to make myself at home as I sat in the lounge and then informed me that she was off upstairs to sort herself out. I genuinely thought she meant to get changed as we planned to go and grab some food. But, the next thing, I heard what I thought was a hair dryer going off. She shouted for me to join her upstairs. Innocently, I didn't think anything of it, but when I entered her bedroom! Oh! My!

There she was playing with herself with a vibrator. Now, you are probably wondering what I did next. Did I take one for the team? The answer is no! I didn't! By now I was pretty sure this *Disney Land Princess* had already exhausted Aladdin, shagged all seven dwarves, sat on Pinocchio's face and got him to lie, and then done Mickey and Goofy. This was no

Cinderella; she was more like Sinerella! We went for some food after this but to say it was awkward was an understatement. Horrifically, I had time to kill until the train home so had no choice.

The other time I travelled was to London. I met a lovely lady, but again the whole experience was not really worth the rail fare. My first impression was a disappointment as she looked nothing like her profile picture – and that to me is a big turn-off. But what I couldn't get my head around was that she just seemed to be away with the fairies. For some reason, when talking her head constantly nodded like the Churchill dog from the TV advert. I should give her some dues though as she was very entertaining. She turned up in a jumpsuit and joked she hoped she didn't need to go toilet as she'd have to take the *whole bloody thing off!* I'm not a designer, but I'm not sure why those jumpsuits don't have poo flaps. Anyway… She was certainly not the high-flying executive she claimed to be; instead she was a stay-at-home mum.

That was lesson learnt for me. When contacting ladies, you will find most these days just will not travel far for love. So, there's no point messaging/winking someone a long way from you as it's likely not to go anywhere.

Chapter 16: First Dates

Or, on when your mother taught you not to

talk to strangers

First dates can be stressful. They are nerve-wracking even when you have previously met and know there is some chemistry that has led to the impending event. Typically, your heart might thump like a woodpecker whacking a mallet against your ribs; your stomach might feel like you've drunk the water in a foreign country, and you might lose motor functions, making simple movements clumsy and embarrassing. But meeting people you have met online is a whole new level of stress.

Please don't consider me lacking in romance; I love a bit of romance. Who doesn't love first kisses, the electricity of fingers touching together, the heat of realising you're both well and truly into each other? But experience has now taught me that the order of romance has changed a little in the digital world.

Initially, I did go to first dates filled with hope and joy: conversations on the phone had got the butterflies dancing, and I was definitely a believer in finding love online. But first dates lose their romance when you go on lots of them. They become a business transaction, where your first date is more like an interview, checking if the person matches their CV.

So, you simultaneously become the interviewer and the interviewee. Gone is the tingly romance, candlelight and the chinking of glasses. In comes planned questions to compare answers, good lighting to check they are who they said, and sobriety to enable swift exits when needed.

But that does mean making it to a second date is the new first date.

In the spirit of honesty, and to share examples of the highs and lows of first dates, let me take you through some of my experiences.

Lesson 1: Sometimes, the problem is you...

Don't get me wrong – I don't think I am the perfect date. For all the stories I regale to you, I'm sure there are women across the South West who can tell tales about me too.

For example, one very good date was laced with micro-embarrassments. These started at the very beginning, as I broke one of the rules of good impressions by arriving early – very early! My date lived near Plymouth; well, to be fair (to me, I'm trying to make excuses), just outside right on the border to

Cornwall, which is a fair drive, but I completely misjudged the timing. I was due to arrive at 5pm, however, I got there at 4.15pm. I tried calling the lady to say I was early but, typically, there was no mobile phone signal in such a rural location. Not wanting to look too keen or – worse – rude, I sat in the car for a few moments. But then, feeling a bit weird sitting in a car outside a lady's house, I plucked up the courage to go and knock on her door. There was no reply, and for a moment I wondered if I'd got to her house before her. So, I did the awkward caller thing and looked through the glass door. I could see the staircase, the landing at the top of the stairs and the bathroom door was wide open. Now, at this point I looked away, but in the turning of my head, many things happened really quickly. Just inside the wide-open bathroom door, I spotted my date. She was getting ready. Fully naked.

The whole thing only lasted a few seconds, but it felt like a lifetime.

And then she clocked me.

At this point, I made matters even worse by ducking down to hide, as if my new invisibility would render my face at the window equally invisible. But instead I looked like a pet dog hiding after doing something naughty. Or worse, like a Peeping Tom.

Boldly, she wrapped a towel around her and sauntered down to the door. "You're early." She noted the obvious but only hinted at the awkward moment that just occurred. "Have you been waiting long?" I didn't know if she was asking out of typical British politeness or trying to work out how long I'd been looking through the window at her naked body.

"No!" I over-stated. "I literally just arrived!"

I should have stopped talking there. And I don't know why I didn't. I think I was attempting to reclaim the impression of decency, or perhaps it was just embarrassment. But I continued: "I just saw you naked through your door," I burbled, "which I'm not sure you're supposed to do on a first date."

She just looked at me with horror!

This might surprise you now, but the date in question went extremely well. We shared food, wine and laughter. Perhaps early nudity is a good ice breaker. She offered for me to stay the night, so perhaps early nudity is a good sign in general... or perhaps she was being a kind host due to the distance I had travelled, and because we'd ended up enjoying a few glasses of wine. At the end of the night we slept in the same bed, however nothing happened sexually between us. We did indulge in a bit of intimate kissing though, which was lovely. And, as you know already, kissing on a first date is rare for me. So, I can hear you ask, how is this an example of a bad date? Well...

The scene was set early in the evening, as my date decided to cook for us before we went out. She had prepared a Mexican dish which was pretty spicy, but I thought nothing of it until we were lying in bed. As we cosied up, and I realised we'd had a nice time, I suddenly felt a tightening in my tummy. The horror! I realised I had a case of trapped wind! I was a pair of bellows about to blow! I was a ticking stink bomb! And I knew it!

It's always awkward getting naked with someone and sharing a bed for the first time as you want to look like you don't have any strange habits. But there was no avoiding this build up. I could feel one big fart brewing in the departure lounge, and there was no way of keeping it in all night. But I also thought I couldn't just let it off while lying next to her. So, I hatched a plan. As naturally as I could, but it was probably pretty awkward really, I said to her, "I just need to whizz out to the car just to grab my mobile phone so I can set my alarm for the morning." And I rushed out of the room, squeezing my butt cheeks together.

While out getting my phone, I released the fart, and felt my fear dissipate in equal measure. I'd cleared the back log so to speak, and I felt so much better for it.

Confident and back in her room, we fell asleep lying in each other's arms. I'm sure you can imagine the cuteness. Time passed, and sleep took over, and my body relaxed. You know when you're soundly asleep and your whole body just relaxes and your breathing slows down, and you have no control over your body movements any more… Well, at this wonderful point, I accidentally let out an almighty fart. Not only did it wake up the lady next to me, but I think it woke the next-door neighbours too.

Well, I didn't know what to do, so I just pretended to still be asleep! Anyway, it's better out than in, even if it's not the first and lasting impression you want to make as a trumpet sleeper. On a related note, an ex of mine used to refer to farting as Love Puffs though, which makes them sound a lot nicer than they are.

Lesson 2: Less is More

One of the scariest moments in my life, apart from the finger-up-the-bum moments, was when I arranged to meet a younger woman I had met online. She was only 27, which was quite a bit younger than me, but she seemed really nice when we chatted online. We arranged to meet in a bar in Weston-Super-Mare, her profile name was "Wonder women from Weston" and everything seemed fine at first, but then I did begin to Wonder if she really was a women.

But then, when we met face to face, she changed from comfortable introductory topics to very personal information. Trying to be less judgemental, I didn't let it bother me that she had two belly buttons and disclosed she had fake boobs in the first few minutes of chatting. I also overlooked that she spoke in a surprisingly deep voice, although I suppose it's fair to say a deep voice isn't an unpleasant thing. But I must admit I did look for an Adam's Apple just in case she was a Steve instead of an Eve… I thought, if this was to work we'd have to work on her pillow talk. I imagined her whispering sweet nothings to me when in bed and it was unsettling; I'm pretty sure her sounding like a man probably wouldn't do it for me!

We met at 4pm and it ended up being quite easy to overlook her rapid openness as she was very easy to talk to, and I got used to the deep voice after a while (it turned out she had undergone a throat operation previously which had damaged her vocal cords). But there was no escaping that she opened up a little more than you should on a first date. And I mean, no escaping. It would appear the more she drunk she got, the more open she was.

Verbal incontinence continued. After the third glass of wine, she told me that her last boyfriend tried to kill her and that she once caught her dad with a hooker. Both moments that perhaps required a longer conversation and left me a little stunned. I didn't know what to say, but the quieter I was, the more she talked. She was slurring her words and was not really making any sense, so decided to bring things to a close. Waiting for a pause in the drunken monologue, I sighed and picked up my keys, "Let's call it a night," I offered. "Let me get you a taxi home."

But she wasn't happy with this. Instead, she demanded I gave her a lift home. I didn't mind too much as it wasn't far out of my way and I was concerned to make sure she got home safely, but I wouldn't normally recommend lift giving or taking on a first date because of *stranger danger*. But as soon as she got into my van and I started driving, she changed into some kind of wild cat! In her deep voice, she repeatedly demanded, "Pull over!" I didn't; stranger danger alert buzzing in my head, I decided to get the drive over and done with as quickly as possible.

Then, she took her clothes off and tried to unzip my trousers. I squirmed away from her, telling her to stop. But then she started playing with herself, all the while instructing me to "Pull over!" as she wanted sex! All I could think of was some words of wisdom my dad gave me, "It's okay to have a large appetite as long as you eat at home."

I'd never been in a position like this before; I mean, who tries to suck a bloke off only three hours after meeting him? If you know the answer to that question, you've probably met the same woman. I didn't take advantage of her, although I'm not sure it could've been described as me taking advantage if anything had happened. I think perhaps I'd have been the victim! Feeling embarrassed and freaked out, I asked her to put her clothes on. Well, it was another jumpsuit – which she seemed to take off with ease; all that baloney about it being awkward going toilet when wearing one – I was no longer convinced. I was thinking: *Blimey! I can see why her ex wanted to strangle her!*

I dropped her back home, and still not picking up on my *no means no*, she invited me into her home. I declined, and I have never doubted that was a wise move.

She texted the next day and was full of remorse. If I'm honest, I genuinely felt sorry for her. I fear for what experiences she has had that means she felt the only way she could get and keep a man was to behave like that. I know she was 13 years younger than me, and perhaps I'm a little old-fashioned, however it was a real eye opener! My mates said she sounded the perfect girl – and I sincerely hope they were joking. My more sensible friends thought she was a nutter, and probably had more diseases than a WHO research facility.

Lesson 3: You can end a bad date early – just be polite

Sometimes a date needs to come to an end a lot earlier than you might have planned. It might seem rude, but it saves hurting feelings in the long run, and it saves wasting anyone's time. For example, I went on one date where our whole conversation was lost in translation. I met a lovely lady from Latvia online and we arranged to meet in the lovely Devon town of Exmouth. She was ridiculously good-looking but a little smaller than I was expecting, not that her petite stature was a problem. That said, this was the shortest date I have ever been on – and again, I'm not referring to her height.

She was polite and friendly – as far as I could work out, anyway, as I couldn't understand a word she was saying. It was less of an accent issue, and more of a lack of common language issue. The whole time we sat there, she spoke only one phrase over and over again. Repeatedly, she asked, "You like rock music?"

I know some people might say it was a bit rude only staying for one drink, however, I am at a stage in my life where I don't want to waste people's time.

Lesson 4: Getting rid of awkward dates

Ladies (or fellas) if you are on a date and you never want to see them again, here is my advice. It's a good tip – but don't crack it out too often, or the nutters will cotton on. When you want to bring the date to a close, give the bloke (or lady) a little hug and hold him (or her) a little longer until it becomes a little weird and then whisper in his (or her) ear, *'I'll never leave you…'*

It will work a treat.

Lesson 5: Be prepared

There are many ways to develop a sound dating routine. I've heard from one woman that she always go to the same bar for the first meeting, so the wining and dining can't bias her first impression. It also means she has got to know the barmen, so they help her escape bad dates with pre-organised drink orders or statements that indicate quietly she wants to get out of an awkward situation.

Personally, I now go on first dates with relatively low expectations – after all, these are less first dates and more first meets – so I have found a way to make the event less pressurised. These days I have a pre-saved text in my phone which says: "Thanks for nice night, don't see it going anywhere but all the best for the future."

Although, I have just realised maybe I should stop using the word NICE! It is a sure sign of getting old when you start dropping *that* word into phrases, for example, I must have a NICE cup of tea or a NICE sit down!

Lesson 6: Listen

I generally find it incredibly easy to talk to strangers; this is a bizarre truth as I was painfully shy as a kid up until the age of 12. The defining change being when I joined the Bird-Gees, the church boy band I told you about at the beginning of the book. Apparently, for me fame was a good antidote to shyness. Our routines to the classic hymns drove the old ladies wild. The number of times puddles could be seen underneath them when we performed was unreal. There is an argument they could have just pissed themselves with laughter.

Originally, shyness used to get the better of me. I remember I was never chosen to play leading roles in the school nativity play; one year I played a donkey – it was pretty low budget – I just had a set of ears and I had to walk across the stage clapping together coconut shells. I think my teacher had been watching too much Monty Python. Eventually, I did work my way up to a speaking part when I was ten. That year, I played the innkeeper. I only had one line to say but as the consummate professional, I can still remember it to this day: "There is no room at the inn."

My dad went to see his grandchildren perform recently in a school nativity; apparently the school did a modern take on the birth of Jesus. My dad said he didn't mind the fact the shepherds were wearing trainers and that one of the wise men was wearing a baseball cap. What he took offence to was that Buzz Lightyear had rocked up in Bethlehem!

Coming back to the present, all my years of online dating has helped me become more confident with talking to strangers and breaking the ice. Although I've never understood how *breaking the ice* is a good metaphor for getting to know someone. I guess it has something to do with *warming up* or *thawing something out*; but it always leaves me in mind of breaking through a frozen lake – and that is something I never want to do! Anyway, the easiest thing to remember when talking to a new person is to ask questions. If the person is shy and nervous, asking questions will evaporate long silences and get them to talk about the subject they know best: themselves. You don't need to spend all night talking about yourself. As my dad always says: *we have two ears and one mouth so we should listen twice as much as we talk.* Everyone has a story to tell.

Lesson 7: Be aware of your audience

Listening can help you understand what your date likes, and it is also a chance for you to know how well you connect. It is important to not use your listening skills for evil: manipulation and false impressions to get someone into bed, for example, are wholly frowned upon (for more advice in that area, read books by D. Trump or H. Weinstein). However, you can and should make sensible adjustments to your behaviour for politeness. For example, I can compare two dates with different teachers to show how one woman got it wrong, and in the other I got it so badly wrong! Incidentally, both dates were with teachers and both deal breakers were to do with our mouths…

For a while I attracted teachers, and this always surprised me as I was thick as pig shit at school. My third and fourth dates were with women from this profession. Luckily, they didn't know each other. One wanted to see me again and the other I never heard from ever again! I think my mouth got me into trouble.

The first teacher seemed quite normal, pleasant to talk to and we had a fun evening. However, at the end of the date, I went to kiss her on the cheek and instead she licked me like a Labrador. She totally took me by surprise, and I thought, *Back the truck up, buddy, no tongues on first dates.* She wasn't really my type (if that is such a thing) and I felt she just saw me as a bit of rough. But I think you should never test the depth of water with both feet, so her tongue lapping was a violation and it made her seem far too keen. It's strange though as she didn't look like a window-licker; she came across almost prim and proper which just goes to show, you should always expect the unexpected.

Teacher number two again was similar in many ways, and she was obviously very educated. I felt our intelligence levels were miles apart. She told a few anecdotes about teaching, including telling me about the issues at her school and that two 12-year-old girls were pregnant. I was shocked! Nothing like that happened when I was a kid! So, I confessed I might have done the odd bit of fingering but that was about it, but it certainly kept me out of pregnancy trouble. Joking, I told her she should teach the kids fingering in assembly. Well, good grief! I might as well have told her I had murdered someone as the look on her face was priceless! She said, "Excuse me?" as if she hadn't understood, and I didn't take the hint that this might not be funny and to retract the joke. So, instead, I repeated it: "Maybe you should teach the kids fingering in assembly." This time I included actions...

I was only trying to help; it is safe to say I never heard from her again.

Lesson 8: Accept that first dates do not equal definite romance

First impressions last and many aspects of these impressions are unavoidable. Sometimes, you meet people who live such different lives, you would never been a match. I admit, there have been times when I have met ladies and before I even get to speak to them, I have been put off.

For example, I once picked up a lady from her house in Newton Abbott, and while driving through the estate I passed cars on bricks. When I got to her house there was a sofa in the front garden. I thought, *For God's sake! Here we go. Welcome to Broken Britain!* When I rang the doorbell, to my horror, it played the Dukes of Hazzard theme tune! Then, my date casually popped out in what I can only describe as *F@ck Me Boots* that stretched right up to her armpits.

"I'm Tracy," she said. I thought, *I'm off.*

Another memorable first impression was when I drove all the way to Torrington. I thought I was lost and drove for ages trying to find her house. Then to my surprise, it turned out she lived in a field in a caravan. It wasn't quite My Big Fat Gypsy Wedding as she was pretty slim, but let's just say, I didn't buy any lucky heather from her or stay that long either.

It didn't help she had quite a few teeth missing and spoke in a dialect which was alien to me.

Some Golden Rules of Online Dating First Dates

Always get the lady to pick location and time, somewhere where she feels comfortable. It might seem sexist, but it's important to make sure your date feels safe. One lady once drove 50 miles to meet me in a pub local to me! Her theory was that if I was a stalker, I wouldn't follow her home.

Pre-warn a mate you are meeting someone. Then, if you go missing, there's someone who knows your last actions and location. But more likely, if it's going badly, text your mate to call you and claim there is a family emergency so you can't stay. I once had a friend call me and told me his budgie had died and I had to come home asap.

Never eat on the first date either as you will be stuck there until all food has been served whether you are having a good time or not. If things are going well, you can always head to Nando's.

NEVER kiss on a first date. The code of conduct at the end of the night is to give the lady a kiss on a cheek and no dry humping!

First impressions always last so when meeting people for the first time, you should always be conscious of what you are wearing and make sure clothes are clean and look the best as you want them to. Don't worry – I don't mean you have to iron creases into your jeans.

Chew gum on the way to make sure your breath smells fresh.

Don't take it too seriously; if you go on these dates with realistic expectations that you are meeting someone new rather than the potential love of your life, you will be less nervous and pressurised.

Don't do the whole game-playing thing; after the first date if you like him or her, tell him or her. If you don't see it going anywhere, say. Nobody likes waiting and gambling on the for the whole, *will he text, won't he text* thing. So don't play games; game playing is for kids.

But again, don't appear too pushy if you do like her; if you want to see her again, let her be the one to decide when. Coming across too keen will push her away, so definitely don't fall into the trap of multiple texts or calls with no reply.

Another great thing I do in the build-up to a first date is I normally text a random fact about myself each day leading up to the date. In most cases the lady will do the same thing. It gives you both something to talk about from the word go when you meet. Plus, it's a great way of getting to know each other a little bit better. But make sure that you leave the facts with lots of unanswered questions to generate curiosity. My facts have included:

I was once in a boyband.

I do not like cheese.

I've had two fingers up my bum – not at the same time.

I have a cat with Down's Syndrome called Dave.

As you can see, I'm a riot. God knows why I'm still single.

CONCLUSIONS: A NEW HOPE

So here we are, near the end of the book. I'm not sure if anyone will ever dress their kid up to look like me for World Book Day, but if they do, I would like them to have a pigeon on their shoulder and a cat with his head stitched back on in their arms.

Now, I appreciate you might think I am anti-online dating after all of these experiences. I am not! Online dating can work, it just hasn't worked for me. And if it hasn't yet for you, I don't want you to feel alone. Plus, it's sad that even though everyone is accessible these days with online dating, nobody really communicates anymore. We've stopped making contact in old-school ways.

It's very easy to lose all hope when you are single, however, I have some final words of hope for you: I mean, everyone has hope in a world where even Rose West, the convicted serial killer, was able to re-marry.

I told you I'd cheer you up and give you hope.

And don't fall for the cheesy stuff. Like, have you ever questioned romantic clichés like when people say, 'I love you to the moon and back'? I have never really understood this saying. The moon is 238,000 miles away, so technically the person is declaring their love for a maximum of 476,000 miles – which isn't that far when you think about it – and would take you 145 days each way in a car without stopping, and probably a bit longer in a yellow metro.

Anyway, I hope you find your happy ending, whatever that may be, but please just remember it's better to be left on the shelf than be in the wrong cupboard.

ABOUT THE AUTHOR

Matt Bird – a unique, funny and successful 40-odd-year-old (anyone would think he wrote this). Almost like a performing seal, except smelling of fish. His romantic history to date – four serious relationships; none of these began online. He never married or had kids; he has only had one and half one-night stands. Two fingers up the bum, thankfully not at the same time.

He lives alone with his cats – Smirnoff and Dave – in a small rural town in Devon with a population of 30,000… yet only five different surnames.

Let's just say in his town all the good girls are all taken – the ones that are left, are single for a reason. Like being in a night club when the lights come on at the end of the night – there's a reason why these girls haven't pulled. Wounded antelopes spring to mind.

After yet another failed relationship, and against his father's advice: "Don't go looking for love, let love come to you," he turned to online dating.

28828027R00140

Printed in Great Britain
by Amazon